RAISING

MOTIVATED KIDS

inspiring enthusiasm for a great start in life

School Savvy Kids Series

cheri fuller

OUR GUARANTEE TO YOU

We believe so strongly in the message of our books that we are making this quality guarantee to you. If for any reason you are disappointed with the content of this book, return the title page to us with your name and address and we will refund to you the list price of the book. To help us serve you better, please briefly describe why you were disappointed. Mail your refund request to: Piñon Press, P.O. Box 35002, Colorado Springs, CO 80935.

www.pinon.org

PIÑON PRESS and the PIÑON PRESS logo are registered trademarks of Piñon Press. Absence of ® in connection with marks of Piñon Press or other parties does not indicate an absence of registration of those marks.

ISBN 1-57683-601-0

Cover photo by Photodisc and Corbis
Cover design by David Carlson Design
Creative Team: Rachelle Gardner, Arvid Wallen, Kathy Mosier, Glynese Northam

Content was originally included in *Motivating Your Kids from Crayons to Career: How to Boost Your Child's Learning and Achievement Without Pressure* by Cheri Fuller, Honor Books, 1990.

Some of the anecdotal illustrations in this book are true to life and are included with the permission of the persons involved. All other illustrations are composites of real situations, and any resemblance to people living or dead is coincidental.

Fuller, Cheri.
  Raising motivated kids : inspiring enthusiasm for a great start in life / Cheri Fuller.
    p. cm. -- (School savvy kids series)
  Includes bibliographical references.
  ISBN 1-57683-601-0
  1. Motivation in education. 2. Education--Parent participation. I. Title.

LB1065.F82 2004
370.15'4--dc22

                                    2004007372

Published in association with the literary agency of Alive Communications, Inc., 7680 Goddard Street, Suite 200, Colorado Springs, Colorado 80920.

Printed in Canada

1 2 3 4 5 6 7 8 9 10 / 08 07 06 05 04

This book is dedicated to Noah and Luke Plum,
my grandsons.

contents

acknowledgments

Heartfelt thanks to:

My editor, Rachelle Gardner, and the terrific NavPress staff.

Parents and teachers: Melanie Hemry, Lynn Fuller, Joanna Smith, Gordon Corbett, Dr. Carol Kelly, my brother George Heath, my sister Marilyn Morgan, Dr. Arthur Bodin, Dr. Jeff Smith, Mrs. Edith Schaeffer, Karen Gale, Kay Bishop, Connie Baker, Marilyn Phillips, and Debbie Leslie.

Dorothy Corkille Briggs, Dr. Priscilla Vail, Dr. Howard Gardner, Louise Bates Ames, and Dr. David Elkind for your research and writings. I benefited from all of you, both as a parent and as a teacher.

And many thanks to all the parents, teachers, and children who shared their experiences and ideas with me.

what is motivation?

One of the biggest concerns I hear from parents and teachers across the country is, "How do we motivate our children?" As parents, we want our children to be the best they can be. We have high hopes for them. We want them to be inspired for learning, for achievement, and for success in life. But despite our best intentions, many kids are unmotivated. In our efforts to boost their motivation, many of us are pushing our kids too far and too fast, and they're becoming burned out. How do we learn the difference between pushing our kids toward burnout and genuinely helping them to be motivated? My desire to solve this dilemma led me to write this book.

When I taught creative writing to elementary-age kids, I was struck by their great expectations for the future. Some were interested in gaining fame and fortune as movie stars; others sought adventure and travel, hoping to go around the world and learn other languages. Some desired a career in sports, wanting to be great basketball players like Shaquille O'Neal or to win a gold medal in the Olympics. Some of their dreams were fanciful—wanting to take a ride in a hot-air balloon, see it snow on the Fourth of July, or invent a roller coaster that would go faster than the speed of light.

And many of the children's hopes were serious:

- "I will stop all drugs!"

- "I will make lots of money and pay all my grandma's bills."

- "I will help the homeless."

The children's writings also reflected their interests in careers and their goals for what they would like to be when they grew up:

- "I'm going to be a biologist and study snakes."

- "I'm going to be a doctor and find a cure for cancer."

- "I'm going to be a writer and publish children's books."

- "I'm going to be an astronaut and explore Venus and Mars."

- "Someday I'm going to be just like my dad!"

Architects, nurses, teachers, scientists, and parents. As I considered all these kids inspired by their dreams, I thought, *How can we—parents and teachers—help kids stay motivated to meet the challenges that lie ahead? How can we equip them to realize all of their wonderful plans?*

motivation: what does it look like?

A national television program I watched a long time ago had a huge impact on me. The show was focused on motivating children for school achievement. Four young boys and their moms sat on a stage, ready to be interviewed.

"Why didn't you make better grades?" the boys were asked.

"I dunno," answered the sixth grader.

"Why didn't you do your homework?" queried the host. "Don't you know how important an education is?"

Their answers were similarly vague—until they were asked, "What's your favorite subject?"

"Lunch!" they quickly responded. "PE!"

I cringed as the report cards of two of the boys were flashed on the television screen, revealing failing grades. The kids' faces fell, their humiliation complete.

Then the boys' frustrated mothers were interviewed.

"What did you do to try to motivate your son to do better?" they were asked.

"Well, I grounded him, took away his bike and after-school playtime, and made him sit and do his homework," the first mother responded. "But his grades didn't get any better."

"What did you do to try to get your son to make better grades?" the second mother was asked.

"I nagged," she replied. "I threatened bodily harm and I carried out my threats. I took away his dessert."

"I talked to his teacher and told her to get tough," another mother added. "I took away his PlayStation and Game Boy."

An educational consultant came on stage next to offer the distraught mothers some expert advice. "Have a study desk, materials, and quiet during study time," he counseled. "Make your children do their homework, even if they have to sit there all evening."

"But I've done that!" mother number two protested. "It never worked."

Although the intentions of those who produced that program were good, I wondered why they hadn't highlighted all the positive ways children can be motivated for learning and achievement—*without* threats, *without* pressure, and *without* bodily harm!

a motivated learner

What is motivation? For me, it's an inner drive that causes me to do something. My motivation may come from a personal desire (for example, to equip and encourage parents), or it may come from an outside incentive (if I finish the book, I'll get a check). When you motivate someone, you inspire hope in him. You stimulate him to action or propel him forward.

When we talk about motivated kids, we're referring to children who have caught a feeling of excitement about learning and accomplishing things. They're enthusiastic about the task at hand—whether at home or at school. They may be self-starters—students who take the initiative to undertake class assignments without reminders or make their beds and clean their rooms without being asked. Or they might need a little more adult involvement but once prodded tackle a job wholeheartedly. If they hit an obstacle or don't understand a concept, they seek help. They don't give up just because a challenge is difficult, but rather have the inner fire to keep going in spite of setbacks. They keep plugging away until the light comes on.

At this point you may be thinking, *Who are these kids? I've never met them!* I hope that after reading this book, you'll have the tools to help your own children become motivated kids.

According to psychologist Carol Dweck, "Motivation is often more important than initial ability in determining our success."[1] Obviously, we're rightly concerned about our kids' motivation levels. So how can we motivate our children without pressuring them? How can we whet their appetites for knowledge and encourage their desire to understand the world around them? How can we ignite the spark within our children that will propel them to embrace their responsibilities—everything from doing their homework and chores to minding their manners? What can we do to encourage the carpe diem mindset, one that perseveres in spite of obstacles and challenges?

Children are naturally curious and come into the world motivated—eager to learn, touch, explore, question, discover. How do we fan the flame of that innate motivation rather than extinguish it?

As parents, we can provide activities and structure our homes in such a way that our kids develop enthusiasm for doing the right thing. Think about how we, as adults, stay motivated to accomplish the things that need to get done. We all have things we're excited about and other things we do just because we have to. What keeps us going? Often it's our relationships that inspire us: We may not love cooking dinner, but we love our family, so we not only cook the meal but put some thought into it as well. We may be motivated by a good example, one that was set for us by a mom, dad, or favorite teacher. Some of us are motivated by our own high expectations of ourselves.

Just like adults, children can develop motivation for all the necessary things in life. No matter how they're wired or what their abilities are, there are many ways we can help our kids get started, build up steam, and go the distance in this marathon of growing up. Throughout the rest of this book, we'll be looking at ways to help our kids build their inner resources of motivation.

our part: developing momentum, boosting motivation

For most parents, spending time cheering for their kids as they play sports is part of the job description. One thing I've noticed as I've spent time in the bleachers is how important momentum is to the outcome of a game. Our son's football coach once told the players how the game of life is much like football: You've got to block your fears, tackle your problems, and whenever you get the chance, head for the goal and score all the points you can!

Growing up does have some similarities to football, especially in the area of momentum. When our son Chris was a student, my husband and I attended a University of Oklahoma football game against Texas Christian University. Oklahoma had a huge opening-game crowd and a great new head coach. They were pumped up to win the game.

Unfortunately, in the first few minutes of the game, TCU got a quick field goal off an interception. Soon after, Oklahoma fumbled and TCU scored again. They were hot! Oklahoma kept trying, but a few penalties and a fumble derailed their efforts. TCU kept gaining momentum until they had the upper hand, and they won the game twenty to seven. Fortunately, in the next few years, Oklahoma's team gained momentum and won the national championship.

What does that football game have to do with your child growing up? Let's look at a typical school year. In September, your child is at a starting point, just as both teams are at the beginning of a game. Perhaps you have expectations of a great year of learning, and your kid is looking forward to fun and new friends. If an interesting subject sparks your child's motivation, if the teacher takes an interest in him and a good relationship builds, or if he makes a few good grades right out of the chute, positive momentum for learning grows. But if every task is grueling, if he fails on assignments and tests, or if he consistently doesn't finish his work for fear it won't be perfect, then the wind can go out of his sails. When a downward spiral gets going, momentum is lost and can be difficult to recover.

This book is all about building motivation and momentum in your child. In the first section of the book, we'll look at the building blocks of motivation: the power of relationship, positive role modeling, expectations, and a healthy perspective on grades. In the second section, we'll cover motivation boosters that bring out the best in your child. In the last part of the book, we'll tackle motivation busters and how to overcome them.

Motivation, the precious spark within each child, can be nurtured at home—not just in the area of schooling but also for life, church, chores, and responsibilities. So let's look at all the ways we can kindle, not dampen, the fires of motivation in our children.

Part 1

the building blocks
of motivation

the first building block: relationship

Carol, an Arizona mom, included her teenage daughters in as many of her activities as she could to expose them to a variety of experiences and to discover their interests. They went together to art museums, on nature hikes, to the library and zoo. They did inner-city mission trips, stargazed in the summer, and planted a garden together. These shared interests carried them through the junior high years and beyond, providing fun memories as well as common ground. They discovered that doing things together was the best backdrop for developing a loving, close relationship and for conversations about peer pressure, guys, faith, and other growing-up issues.

Each of them enjoys reading, and Allison (nineteen), Andrea (fourteen), and Carol now have their own mother-daughter book club. They take turns choosing the title of the month and then discuss it over lunch at a restaurant. It not only has led to some interesting conversations, but both girls are also motivated about life and learning, in and out of the classroom.

Like Allison and Andrea, motivated children tend to be those who have close, loving relationships with their parents. If the parent-child relationship is weak, all the enriching academic programs and school reforms will not necessarily result in motivated kids who are interested in learning. Unmet emotional needs can block learning in children. The child starved for love, acceptance, and attention from her parents has scant energy to face the challenges of school and life.

Studies of the most motivated students in a California high school showed that those who were doing well and had high goals and achievement records were the ones whose parents had stayed involved with them from their early years through their high school career. The parents of successful students were engaged with their children. They talked about things the kids were doing. They resisted the temptation to provide their children with a lot of early freedom in dating and driving. They were not inordinately harsh or overprotective but established clear boundaries of behavior. They showed a real interest in their children's lives in school and out. They made parenting a priority, spending a great deal of time with their children.[1]

A secure parent-child relationship is a major foundation for a child's self-worth. With a positive view of themselves, kids become more motivated, take risks needed for learning and achievement, and keep working toward those goals even in the face of frustration and setbacks.

Our children will encounter people outside the family who will put them down or give them negative feedback. They may go through hurtful or difficult experiences, but their time spent at home will set the stage for whether they will establish and maintain healthy, positive patterns of behavior or negative, destructive ones. One of the ways we can help kids feel loved and worthwhile is to establish a strong, loving relationship with them.

what's it all about?

One day I dropped my daughter off at a babysitting job and then took my son and his friend to play basketball. I was on my way home to prepare dinner and was feeling like a glorified cook-chauffeur. A thought occurred to me (Doesn't some of your best thinking take place alone in the car or bathtub?): *What's parenting all about?*

Sure, it's about giving birth to a precious baby and the nights spent walking him when he's colicky. It's about spring stroller rides, teething times, toilet training, arranging playdates, and the first day of school. Parenting is about the responsibility of teaching and training, providing, loving, and caring. It includes taking our children to the doctor or dentist, giving them birthday parties, taking them to piano lessons or sports practice. It's fixing hundreds of lunches and helping with homework.

But parenting is more than that.

As our kids grow, it includes operating not only a car pool service, a laundry service, and an educational consulting service, but also a counseling service when there are bad dreams and disappointments. It's open houses and school carnival nights, nursing kids through the flu and colds. Later, it's staying up to wait for them to come home from the senior prom.

But parenting is even more than this, I thought. It's also about building a relationship with our children that will last a lifetime. It involves learning how to listen and how to communicate. It is learning how to love these changing, growing people who are so like us and yet so completely different from us. It is also learning to let go, realizing and accepting that as our children grow, they will develop independence and eventually stand on their own two feet. We may not think about it in the early stages of parenting, but we're raising our kids to leave us.

As a professor once said, the key ingredient in the successful development of a human being is the fact that some adult is crazy about her—crazy enough to put her and her welfare before career, ambitions, the acquisition of things, or a new spouse. Someone is crazy enough about her to take time to build bridges, to form a strong relationship with her.

That someone is you or me—the parent chosen, out of all the people in the world, to guide and nurture a young life.

building bridges

> *It is hard to develop any self-worth without a*
> *close personal link to at least one adult.*
>
> EVE BITHER[2]

Building a relationship with a child is not always an easy task. In the early years, it's easy for us to get busy and miss opportunities for bridge building. When children are little, we're often trying to keep them occupied so we can do the important adult tasks we feel so pressured to take care of.

It doesn't get any easier as our children move into the middle school years and on to high school. Their schedules become so filled that they may have difficulty working *us* in! Often what's missing is a *bridge*—some common ground both parent and child can relate to, something they can both enjoy doing together.

A bridge is something that provides a connection or contact, something that spans or links. In the parent-child relationship, a bridge is built brick by brick, moment by moment during the time the two spend together. And the thing that helps—the key to building this connection—is finding something that both parent and child are interested in, enjoy doing, and can share.

"It's important to be doing something *together,* not just something *for* the child, but something you really enjoy; not just as a reward or a duty, but as having found out and discovered something that can be talked about and shared when you're together," says Edith Schaeffer, a mother, grandmother, and great-grandmother and author of *What Is a Family?*[3]

Bridge building is not just doing something for the child in a patronizing way, not just spending time with him because a book says to. Rather, it's sharing an enjoyable moment or a pleasurable activity because you both want to. This activity could be reading aloud a fascinating story, hiking an unknown trail and collecting interesting rocks along the way, playing tennis together, or painting a mural in the garage.

on the golf course

My son Chris loves to golf, and so does his dad, Holmes. But one summer Holmes was working longer hours and had an injury, so his golf playing with Chris was temporarily curtailed. I'd never had any desire to play the game, nor had I ever been on a golf course, except for a power walk.

But Chris was fifteen and not interested in riding bikes, going shopping, talking, or engaging in any of the other feminine pursuits I enjoyed. "Do you want to go and play tennis?" I'd ask. That was up my alley. "Not really," he'd reply.

I wanted to find something we could do together, so I invited Chris to the driving range, where he taught me how to swing the golf club. The next time out, I drove the cart for him. (In the ninety-five-degree heat, this was a real treat considering he usually carried his heavy bag and clubs.) On that late June afternoon I discovered that I loved being out there on the public golf course. I didn't know how to play, but driving the "golf buggy" was like driving a little go-cart. Chris and I sipped sodas, and I took in the variety of trees that we mingled among as we made our way around the fairways. There was a cool breeze off the water, and the sailboats were bright and colorful. We saw a white-tailed bunny, a Canada goose, and an egret. I felt as if we weren't even in the city.

As I watched Chris work on his different strokes, I served as scorekeeper and found myself not just enduring golf for his sake, but enjoying it. Chris is normally quiet, but he opened up and chatted as we drove around the course. He told me his favorite kind of golf ball and described the basic shots I'd need to learn to play the game.

"My putting is good, but my driving is awful," he confided.

"Next time we'll practice at the driving range before you play nine holes," I suggested.

During that afternoon that we spent together, I learned about some of my son's ideas and experiences that I may never have heard about had I stayed home or followed my usual routine. I may never be a good golfer, but I cherish the memories of the outings Chris and I had together that summer.

anchors of security

> *Parents are anchors of security to children.*
> *Parents of secure children spend more time with*
> *them. There is close daily interaction. Close emo-*
> *tional ties are built daily, in small ways. Then*
> *any crisis can be handled. Having faith in their*
> *parents, they have faith in themselves and oth-*
> *ers, and life makes sense to them.*
>
> DR. YAMAMOTO[4]

We all want to build strong relationships with our children, and we know one of the ways we can do this is by talking with them. But we soon realize that the "good talks" don't happen on our timetable. Rather, they happen at moments when we are doing something with our kids—cooking dinner, baking cookies, grocery shopping, writing thank-you notes. Working together can provide opportunities to talk, listen, and just be with one another, no matter what the age of our children.

One mother enjoys scrapbooking with her daughter. Together they shop for supplies, pick out photos, and create scrapbooks of family memories. A dad and his three elementary-age sons decided to take up hunting together, so they took gun safety courses and set aside occasional Saturdays for trips into the mountains. Another mom and her daughters enjoy Saturday mornings at the local bookstore, browsing, sipping hot chocolate, and choosing a book or two. Time together can be spent doing simple things, such as playing Ping-Pong or walking the dog. One dad I know had a standing date with his son every Saturday to go to breakfast together. That weekly time over pancakes helped them keep up with each other's lives.

All these activities may seem obvious, but one thing I've discovered is that in the busyness of life, it's easy to forget to schedule time for these normal, everyday pursuits. Most parents find they need to be intentional about spending time with their children, especially as the kids become teenagers. Try setting a goal of fifteen minutes a day or one shared activity, even if it's brief. Dinner together at the family table (without the television blaring in the background) is a great start. You may also want to set up standing dates to do things individually with your kids on a weekly or monthly basis. One family I know sets aside time every few months for Dad to take each of the children individually for a full-day outing, and Mom does the same. Trips with Dad usually involve hiking, fishing, or snow skiing; trips with Mom are usually along the lines of ice skating, shopping, and going to the movies—but every outing is based on shared interests, not just the interests of the child or parent.

The important thing is to find a way to connect because no matter how simple or ordinary the activity is, it will help build a bridge between the parent and child. Communication naturally flows out of time spent together in an interesting and enjoyable activity.

When communication lines between parent and child are open, learning and motivation are boosted. Kids who do well on mental tests and in schoolwork are more likely to come from homes where there is a great deal of open communication. According to author Dorothy Corkille Briggs, "When parents and children are warmly interested in each other and their activities, when children feel safe to share ideas and feelings, intellectual growth is stimulated."[5]

Sometimes we focus so much on doing things *for* our child that we forget to focus on him as a person. We may be rushing so fast to bake the class cookies, buy his school clothes, and make money for his education that we overlook *him*. Direct involvement tells a child that he is valuable. Being there for him and listening to him, rather than always being preoccupied with adult worries, tells him, "I love you. You are important enough to warrant my presence and my full attention. You matter!"

It may be difficult to see a direct link between all these relationship-building activities and our children's motivation levels. Nevertheless, every aspect of parenting is built upon the relationship we have with our kids. If our connections with our kids are strong and positive, our children are more likely to learn from us, heed our examples, want to live up to our expectations, and build their own set of positive values from which they can find motivation.

the second building block:
a good example

"Mom, this door is so squeaky! We gotta get Dad to fix it!" called four-year-old Lauren as she swung her bedroom door from side to side, listening to the high-pitched sound. Her mom came to look.

"How about we fix it ourselves?" Mom suggested, getting out the WD-40. She showed Lauren how to spray the door hinges and then demonstrated how the squeak had disappeared.

Lauren was impressed. "Cool! Can I do it?"

"Sure," her mom told her. "In fact, why don't you fix all the squeaky doors in the house?"

Off the little girl went, happily spraying all the door hinges, empowered by her newfound capability and motivated by her sense of accomplishment.

Besides providing an opportunity for a fun distraction, when we as parents say, "Let's do it ourselves," we make use of a positive, inexpensive, yet dynamic way of fanning the flame of motivation in our kids. It's a small, everyday way of showing that we're not afraid to jump in and handle things. We demonstrate that we're motivated to solve problems and that doing necessary tasks can be fun. Our kids experience the great feeling of learning something new—one of the most powerful sources of motivation.

Our role modeling is a powerful motivator because the number one way kids learn is by imitation. So one of your most powerful tools in guiding and motivating them is setting a good example.

the power of example

"Action is character," my friend's writing teacher used to say. He knew that although words are important, people's *behavior* says more about who they are. As parents, we send our most powerful messages through our *actions*. Like it or not, kids follow the leader, and for many years, we are the leaders. Have you caught your kids repeating your expressions or imitating your gestures?

We may not feel qualified to be a role model with its implication of excellence or perfection, but kids are always watching what we do. They think what they see us do is okay for them to do too. Gradually through their growing-up years, they incorporate many of our behaviors, attitudes, and actions into their value system.

Countless studies show that whether it has to do with dietary habits, manners, drug use, physical violence, or treating people kindly, one of the major factors that influences children's behavior is parental example. Enter "parental example" into a search engine on the Internet and spend ten minutes perusing the results. You'd be amazed at how much research has been done in an attempt to "prove" the obvious: The example parents set has an enormous impact on children. If you want your kids to be positive and enthusiastic about household chores, you'll need to have that attitude yourself. The best thing you can do to keep your kids interested in school is to let them see you being an active learner. "Motivation happens more in the process of living with a parent who is intellectually alive and shows excitement over the world of books, ideas, numbers—it's contagious!" says Dr. Arthur M. Bodin.[1]

setting the example

My friend discovered grapevines growing thickly in her backyard and decided to learn how to make grapevine wreaths. After reading books and searching the Internet for information, she took on the project with gusto. When your child sees you doing something like this, she learns how to locate information and gains confidence in trying new things. Your actions may motivate your child to dig for more information on things that interest her and can inspire her to try an unfamiliar project that intrigues her.

As another example, consider the subject of reading. One of the main factors that distinguished the homes of every child studied in Delores Durkin's comprehensive research on early readers was that *the parents were avid readers and led their children by example.*[2] "Let your child see you totally enthralled in a novel. Let him hear you laugh as you read the Sunday paper or a magazine," says Jennifer Jacobson, an educational and child development specialist from Cumberland, Maine. "Nothing is so motivating as watching a parent caught in the act of enjoyment. By the time your child learns the magic, the beauty, the adventure of the printed word, he will already have acquired a love for reading."[3]

"Children's brains are not easily fooled," says Frank Smith. "They learn what we *demonstrate* to them, not what we may hope and think we teach."[4] You can naturally demonstrate to your young child the importance of literacy by talking to him while doing something that involves reading or writing: "I'm writing my grocery list so I won't forget the things we need when we go to the store." Whether you are writing checks, reading the classified ads, taking phone messages, or leaving notes, an explanation of your activity will help your child see the purpose of literacy in daily life.

everyday role modeling

If we live a sedentary lifestyle, our kids are more likely to be sedentary and as a result be at a higher risk for obesity. If we exhibit solid morals and character, such as telling the truth and treating people with kindness, our children will soak up those values and be more apt to live by them.

Even in our mistakes we can be good role models. Our willingness to admit our own errors and learn from them is important. This attitude carries over into education and affects children's risk-taking behavior, an important factor in the learning process. Home can be a place where kids get the support they need to try new things and to risk making mistakes in order to grow.

If we allow them the freedom to make mistakes, they won't be as discouraged by their failures. They'll be able to admit their lack of knowledge in a subject yet still be open to learning about it. We can help kids think of mistakes as a way of learning to do tasks better and as a natural part of the learning process.

Ask yourself these questions: *As a parent, how well do I handle failure? How persevering am I in overcoming obstacles, delays, and disappointments in my everyday life?* These are important questions because they represent a crucial factor in our children's motivation. In fact, one vital trait of giftedness is perseverance. Studies show that persistent children tend to become successful adults. Although there are many inborn personality traits that can affect our children's growth and development, the daily example we set when faced with difficulties or problems will speak much more clearly to them than any lectures we might deliver. The fact is that our children's perseverance tends to mirror ours.

One day, for example, Brian's father told him to stick with his math problem until he had found the solution. As Brian worked, he could hear his father in the garage trying to fix the car radio. He had been at it for a week, taking the radio apart, reassembling it, going to the shop to get a part, and then taking it all apart again. Brian learned from his dad's example and found his own perseverance to keep going. He stuck with his math problem.

If you're trying to keep your daughter from quitting the soccer team when she's discouraged because every game ends in defeat, yet you drop out of the choir because you don't like the director, it's doubtful she'll think it's important to be persistent when the going gets rough. This applies to any value or life skill you want to instill. If you want your kids to develop a servant's heart, take them along when you serve at the soup kitchen. If you want them to be caring to others, nurture them with care and loving concern.

Parents are models, but so are relatives, pastors, teachers, community leaders, and adult friends—all can have a positive impact on our children. I'll never forget the motivated fourth grader who shared about the influence of one of his heroes: "My grandfather told my dad who told me that two important things in life are a good name and a good education, and I'm working for both!"

We can look to our extended family, church, and community for good role models for our children. People who have interesting jobs and are excited about them are fascinating to children and can be a great influence. Invite such a person to dinner and let your child learn from him. Perhaps you know someone who is doing heart research, writes songs, or is moving to another country to be a missionary. At age nine, our son Chris was inspired by our friend Dr. Warren Low's description of the new knee joint he had invented. This encouraged Chris's desire to pursue the field of medicine, and he's now a physician. Maybe among your acquaintances there is someone who builds sailboats or creates computer programs. When trying to motivate a child to develop his personal goals, there's nothing better than exposing him to adults who have purpose in their lives and work in interesting professions.

In articles we read in the newspaper or in programs we watch on television, we can point out stories about people who have overcome obstacles. We can share about unsung heroes who have shown great courage, given extra effort, or contributed to the needs of others. There are people all around us who can inspire our children by modeling positive character traits, such as loyalty, devotion to duty, compassion, persistence, and determination.

the third building block:
expectations

Kids who succeed and overcome obstacles in school and life usually have one experience in common: They have at least one person in their life who had high expectations for them and provided support and structure for their dreams. Shavar Jeffries is just one example. When he was eight years old, he was shuttled among family members. When he was eleven, his stepfather murdered his mother. Shavar's teachers called him "at risk." He and his sister moved in with their grandmother, Nancy, who began working nights as a prison guard so Shavar and his sister could attend a private Catholic school because they lived in a bad area. His grandma had high expectations for Shavar's behavior and learning, insisted on homework and reading, and believed that Shavar could achieve. She preached to him that the reward for good grades isn't money or material things but the satisfaction of learning for learning itself.

An A student through his secondary schooling and college, this young man who was failing in elementary school graduated from Duke University with honors and started law school at age twenty-one. He had the inner drive, but it was his grandma who believed in him and provided structure. For that, he'll always be grateful.

Billy also experienced the power of high expectations. As a freshman in high school, he wanted desperately to play football. Although Billy practiced with the team every day, he rarely got to play because he was short, overweight, and so slow that teammates nicknamed him Turtle. He didn't look like a football player, and he sure couldn't run like one.

But Billy's dad had high hopes for him and saw more potential in his son than everybody else did. One day, Billy's dad talked with his son's coach. He told the coach that he believed it was important to draw out the best in every player to help him develop his potential. Billy's dad knew his son didn't look like a great football player, but he tried to envision what Billy would look like in a few years when he was a senior, after he'd grown and developed with good coaching and guidance. He said, "Coach, can you see Billy with an all-American jersey covering his broad shoulders and narrow waist?"

That conversation changed Coach Mitchell. He began seeing kids as they might be, not as they were or are. He saw people's strengths rather than focusing on their weaknesses. In the next four years, Coach Mitchell spent extra time with Billy. By the time Billy was a senior, he'd become a star football player and an all-American.[1]

what are your expectations?

Kids of all ages need parents, teachers, and coaches who believe in them 100 percent, support them, and expect them to do their best.

"My goal for Zachary is that he'll do better and achieve more than I did," says one dad.

"I'd like to see my son improve his handwriting, become a good reader, be happy with his friends and school, and develop more confidence," says another.

"I have the dream that my children are going to be wonderful successes, but I won't do the work for them," stated a mother of five. "It's their job to 'duke it out' day to day, and it's my job to stir up their dreams and to encourage them to accomplish their goals."

What are your expectations for your child? The word *expectation* refers to anticipation, to the act of looking forward to something. Expectation implies a hope or belief about what is going to happen or what someone is going to do in the future. But expectation does more than just anticipate. It has a certain amount of power to predict and produce what is anticipated. Kids are particularly attuned to the expectations of their parents and teachers, and they tend to fulfill them.

This principle of positive expectation produces dramatic results when applied in the workplace or in school. A new supervisor is given a list of six employees and told that they have been especially productive in the past. After a period of time, these workers turn out to be his star performers. Actually, the six have been picked at random. They succeed, not because they are inherently superior, but because they are *expected* to succeed, because they are treated like winners—like valuable, productive employees. The supervisor, anticipating fine work, is not disappointed.

The same powerful effect of positive expectation can be seen in the classroom. Researchers have gone into schools at the beginning of the year, tested the students to determine their academic potential, and then grouped them randomly. Their teachers were then told which of their students had been placed in a group consisting of bright "late bloomers" who had academic promise and would become high achievers. (Actually, their test scores were not outstanding.)

At the end of the term, all the children were tested again. The ones who had been labeled "promising" showed more significant gains in intelligence and achievement than any other group of students in school. Their teachers had expected them to succeed, which had built their confidence in themselves and their abilities. The results also suggested that the teachers' high expectations for these students translated into more positive feedback, more challenging activities, and a boost to the kids' level of learning and achievement.

Parental expectations have an equally strong influence on children. "We know from numerous studies that children usually remain loyal to parental expectations," says school psychologist Dr. Carol Kelly. "If they hear positive expectations—that they will do well, that they can meet the daily challenges, that they will go on to college—then they do better in the classroom."[2] Dr. David Lowenstein agrees: "Confident expectations of success based on your child's potential (not yours) often bring success."[3]

expectations live on

I saw expectations operate in our family while I was growing up. One way I knew I could please my father was to do well in school.

Education was important to him, and all of us children knew it. He'd apparently assessed our abilities and felt we could make high grades if we worked at it. Papa never paid us for getting an A, but I could tell that he was happy with a good report card by the smile that spread across his face. That was reward enough for me.

In his quiet, mostly nonverbal way, Papa let us know that he had high expectations for us. Although he died when I was only eleven and I knew that never again would he preside over the dinner table, come to open house at school, or examine our report cards, the foundation had been laid in me and the power of his positive expectations lived on. I went on working hard, aiming to learn the most and do the best in each of my classes. Consequently, I enjoyed school, liked and appreciated my teachers, and discovered some favorite subjects along the way. The result of my dad's expectations was the development of my confidence in the classroom.

bringing out the best in your child

How can we establish and maintain high but realistic expectations that motivate our children? In order to have reasonable expectations, it's important to gain an understanding of our kids' capabilities, personality, and temperament. Some children will shine in academic work. Others will work hard but never make the honor roll. A child may be great with words but have trouble with numbers, or vice versa. Some kids will excel in music, sports, or computers. Some are late bloomers, and others peak early. Some like the bustle of a busy classroom, while others do best quietly working alone. These special characteristics, skills, and gifts must be taken into consideration in setting expectations.

If we have strong expectations for our son to become a lawyer when he dislikes political science and longs to design space shuttles, we can easily set ourselves up for frustration and disappointment. A friend of mine recalls her high school days when her dad would sit her down and encourage her to excel in math because in his mind, a career in accounting would provide her with a good income, stability, and flexibility. Never mind the fact that his daughter hated math, spent every spare second with her nose in a book, excelled at creative writing, and was on the drama team! If we don't keep our expectations realistic and based on what we know of our children, we risk not only frustration but also damage to the relationship. My friend still looks back on those high school days and remembers the pain of realizing that her dad wasn't paying attention to the very essence of who she was.

Each child has special intelligence gifts, individual strengths, and unique interests. She also has certain character qualities and a learning style that need to be considered in the learning process. (See my book *Talkers, Watchers, and Doers* for ways to discover and develop your child's learning style.) Testing and evaluation at school can provide clues about what a child might achieve in a certain subject such as math or language, but a test is not a foolproof indicator of ability. It gives only clues, not absolute conclusions. Tests can, in fact, be faulty. They should not be used to produce labels to stick on children or limit our view of a child's potential.

More important than standardized tests are your observations about your child: his interests, abilities, talents, and skills. You've been observing your child since birth. You've noticed if he was outgoing or slow to warm up to new people and situations. You know if he's an active, driving kid who struggles to sit down for long periods. You see what he's good at. As he grows, you know how to read his signals about what fascinates him.

You can harness this knowledge to help him become motivated even in difficult tasks, as Valerie, a mom I know, did. When her son Brian was eight years old, he still hadn't learned to read. He had a condition called Williams Syndrome that produced mild to moderate retardation, sensitive hearing, heart disorders, and sometimes, as in Brian's case, a talkative personality. After working with him for several years using every book and curriculum they had, teachers at his special ed school said he just wasn't going to learn to read. But his mom had high hopes for her son that weren't squelched by this bump in the road. She decided to combine one of the strengths of the disorder, a love of language, with her son's big fascination, car washes, to teach him to read.

Valerie read car wash magazines aloud to her son. One night Brian said, "Mom, I'm going to read this magazine by myself someday!" So she made flash cards with car wash words. They strung those words together to make the first sentence he ever read. Sentences became little books, and before long Brian was on his way to becoming a good reader. At age fourteen, he read at a seventh-grade level, excelled in computers, had spoken to thousands of car wash owners at national conventions, and set a goal of owning a car wash business someday. As Norman Vincent

Peale once said, "When expectancy turns the key, great things will happen."[4]

the impact of suggestion

Sometimes we reveal our true expectations through negative suggestions that destroy motivation before it ever has a chance to get going. We might say, "Don't worry about trying to get an A in biology—I was never good at science either." It seems obvious that this might squash a kid's motivation to work hard, but sometimes we find ourselves saying things like this while trying to be helpful. Negative suggestions produce negative thinking, and negative behavior trails right along behind. These pessimistic words can also produce a learned helplessness that discourages the child from trying, either because he's convinced that he'll fail or because he has learned that success really doesn't mean anything. Such downers throw cold water on the spark of motivation. The result is that the child never develops the momentum he needs to keep trying.

Most kids are exposed to far too much negativism, especially those who have any kind of learning difficulty or problem in school. One study showed that by the time a child graduates from high school, she will have heard over fifteen thousand negative words, phrases, or expressions, such as "No," "Don't," "Can't," and "Shut up."[5] Children hear about the wrong things they do much more than they hear about the right. They need positive feedback to counteract the effect of the negatives and to develop and maintain a healthy view of themselves.

Try focusing on improvement and stay away from comments that emphasize your children's errors. Recognize your kids' small successes. A caring Little League coach once told me, "These kids just beam when I point out a little improvement they've made. I always try to reinforce based on improvement and *not* focus on mistakes, especially with the boys who aren't the strongest players or are struggling to keep up with the others. If a teacher, coach, or parent points out any little improvement, it gives the child the confidence he needs to try harder."

You can replace negatives with encouraging expressions, such as "You're improving," "You can figure it out," "Let's look at the problem this way," "You can do it," "I'll help," "Let me show you how," and "That's better." In doing so, you'll find your child becoming more motivated.

avoiding comparison

Last Saturday I was sitting in a large indoor playground at a shopping mall, watching our grandson Caleb play. Two dads next to me held their baby boys.

"How old's your kid?" the first dad asked.

"He just turned six months," dad number two answered.

"So's mine—this week he'll be six months," said the first father.

"Boy, he's *big*—bigger than my little guy," dad number two said.

"The doctor says he's in the ninety-ninth percentile for height. But it's no wonder. I'm six feet two inches."

Dad number two, who looked about five feet seven inches max, looked distressed. "Well, mine's already got four teeth."

"Your baby's ahead of mine. He's only got two teeth," the big dad conceded.

Comparison starts so early. But no two kids are alike, and to compare them can cause problems: "I wish she were organized like her big sister." "I wish Matt made high grades like my friend's son." "Why is my kid always tuned out on the soccer field instead of kicking the winning goals?" As John Drescher says, "Continual comparison builds inferiority feelings that harm personality development."[6] Comparison causes kids to become unmotivated because they begin to feel unaccepted for who they are. Instead of comparing, we can recognize and celebrate each of our kids' different abilities, personalities, and gifts. Most important, our kids need to know that we love them for who they are, not for what they do.[7]

balancing expectations

Balance in any part of our life is difficult to achieve. Many of us tend to go to one extreme or the other—we're either on a radical diet or we eat too much; we overexercise or we're too sedentary. In a similar way, our expectations regarding our kids may be too low or excessively high. We need to find a balance.

Dealing with low expectations. Sometimes because of our own limitations or past school experiences or because of a faulty assessment by a teacher or test, we underestimate our child's abilities.

Low expectations can limit any youngster's progress and destroy her motivation.

Consider what your early experiences of school, sports, and friendships were like and how they've colored your expectations of your child and your assessment of her capability or potential. In the midst of that reflection, remember that your child is an individual. And beware of limiting her possibilities by allowing her to be unfairly labeled by you or the school system. Many times parents and teachers don't expect much from a child who has a learning problem of any kind, even though she may actually be otherwise very gifted.

Dealing with overambition. Sometimes parents' expectations are so high that a child feels he can never measure up. Three As and two Bs on the report card are not acceptable; he must bring home all As. Just participating on the gymnastics team isn't sufficient; they expect their daughter to be number one. In these cases, the parents' own degree of self-worth may rest on what kind of showing their child makes in school and sports activities. When parents continually push their kids to succeed, it may be their own self-image and personal status at stake.

Overambition doesn't really motivate kids. As Dorothy Briggs says, "Remember, overambition comes through to children as *non-acceptance.* Unrealistically high expectations mean strong disappointments. And disappointments slam against self-esteem. They turn off the 'go-power' and then the child doesn't even turn on his engine."[8] Unrealistic expectations often lead kids to stop trying altogether.

When a child fails to meet her parents' unattainably high

expectations, she usually feels discouraged rather than motivated. If you have a tendency toward overambition, you might consider these points:

- As you think about your children, write a list of the different expectations you have for each. Try to evaluate each one individually and objectively. Beside each entry write, "realistic" or "unrealistic," "too easy" or "too difficult." Include what you expect in a variety of areas—school, sports, family relationships, homework, reading, chores, and other activities.

- Talk with your older children about what ambitions *they* think you've had for them. Ask them how well they think they have fulfilled those expectations and how they feel about them. Their answers might surprise you and in any case will shed light on hidden expectations so you can encourage them more effectively. Clarify your real expectations if they have misconceptions.

Parents who encourage their children have positive expectations for them but aren't demanding. When we balance our "great expectations" with a realistic view of our children's ages, abilities, limitations, and needs and when we accept and love them for who they are and not just for what they do or achieve, they're much more likely to develop the courage and motivation they need to undertake new tasks and keep on learning despite difficulties, setbacks, or disappointments.

the fourth building block:
a healthy perspective

Kids have a lot of worries these days. Events over the past few years have opened a Pandora's box for kids. Random shootings in Montgomery County, Maryland; terrorist attacks on the East Coast; war in the Middle East; and children and teens kidnapped in their own homes and neighborhoods—kids have plenty to worry about.[1] Perhaps that's why we find it surprising that one of their biggest worries is grades.

In a survey of eight thousand fifth through ninth graders, students said one of their top worries was grades. Another survey questioned parents about their biggest concern for their teenagers, and again the number one answer was grades.[2]

Schools, in an effort to tighten requirements and improve the quality of education, often increase competition over students' grades. Parents, with a desire for their children to succeed, can unknowingly add to the stress by developing a high-pressure approach to report cards.

For a number of years, Dr. Arthur Bodin served as president of an emergency treatment center that answers the calls of young people in crisis situations in the Los Angeles area. "We see regularly an increase in calls around the first grading period, not when school starts," he says. "Parents get upset about report cards, tempers flare, kids get worried."[3] Often parents overreact to low grades. Social workers, police, and teachers are seeing that report card time can even trigger a wave of child abuse.

Another problem that accompanies grade pressure is cheating. A character survey of 8,600 high school students across the country showed that 71 percent of American teenagers say they cheat on school exams, largely because of a grades-at-any-cost, A-at-any-price attitude on the part of students, pressure from home, and a powerful system of rewards and punishments on the part of teachers.[4]

A Dallas high school principal says,

> Cheating in our high school and many others I'm in touch with is at epidemic proportions. And it's not the C or D students who are cheating. It's the top students who are pressured to stay at the top. To keep in the top quarter of their class in a competitive high school like ours may mean keeping up an average of ninety-six or ninety-seven. We're saying, "You have to keep your grades up to get into good colleges," or "You don't want your class rank to fall." There's no room for a low grade or missed assignment in any subject.[5]

One middle school teacher says, "I see children striving for grades because they are paid more for an A than for a B. Sometimes they will bargain with me for a better grade or cheat. The grade becomes more important than the learning."[6]

Certainly part of the cheating problem is an overall decline in the values and integrity in our society. But some kids cheat because they have a learning disability and struggle to succeed in school. When they get extremely frustrated or are failing, they may think cheating is the only answer. When children become too embarrassed to ask for help, they tend to resort to cheating. Others cheat because they're involved in so many activities that they don't make time to study. Whether a child gets away with cheating or gets caught, it keeps him from learning what he should. If he gets by through cheating instead of studying the material, it will hurt him later when he needs to know the facts.[7]

what kids say about grades

Good grades are great, of course, and it makes parents feel good to see their child at the top of the class. But let's get a perspective on grades and what they really mean. First, what do children say about them?

Third Graders Say:

- "If you don't make As, you don't get to go to college—that's what my mom said!"

- "I like grades when they're good and I get a raise in my allowance."

- "I like to make good grades, and then my parents take me out to eat at Red Lobster!"

- "Sometimes I feel like burning my report card before my parents see it. I don't like it when I open my report card and have to worry about taking it home to Mom and Dad."

- "Sometimes I worry, like if I might get a C. My parents would ground me."

- "When I get a good report card, Mom says, 'I love you' and takes me out to dinner to celebrate."

- "My grandpa gives me a dollar for every A+ I make. That's just an incentive to remind me to do good."

- "I'm sort of afraid that I might make a bad grade because then I couldn't be what I want to be. Because you have to be real smart to be what I want to be—a veterinarian."

- "When I grow up, I want to be in the air force, and you have to have good grades, especially in math, and an A+ in computers to get to go."

Sixth Graders Say:

- "I get excited about making the highest grade because I know I'm going to be pleased with myself and my parents will be happy."

- "I worry about making passing grades because if I don't, I'll be held back and then I'll be with younger kids."

- "I'm worried that if I get a bad grade I'll be disappointed in myself; it would be embarrassing, and my dad would be mad."

- "I'm afraid I'm not going to get enough study time because I always leave everything till the last minute to do, and I'm afraid I'm not going to get it all done. Then I won't live up to my parents' expectations. When I don't get a high enough grade they get mad, but they tell me I can get better."

- "I don't feel pressured about grades because my mom just says to do the best I can and doesn't say get As. And sometimes she quizzes me and helps me study for a test."

Younger kids may not have the faintest notion how a grade is figured or what it stands for. So when parents berate them for bringing home poor grades, they may wonder if grades are something to be feared, like a disease. We need to know what grades mean to our children. If they are not making good grades, they may take the failure personally (as they do most things) and figure they must be bad people. Or they may take their low marks as a form of punishment. They might think that bad grades indicate disapproval or a lack of personal regard—that their teacher has a grudge against them or a dislike for them. If their grades are lower than their classmates', they may feel ashamed or stupid.

the good news about grades

Although report cards seem to exert a big influence on both parents and children, they're actually nothing more than a way to keep records. As Kevin, a third grader I taught, once said, "Grades are a symbol of how you're doing. If you miss turning in papers, that lowers your grade."

Grades don't tell the whole story, though unfortunately we sometimes act as if they do. Whether the grade is an A, a B, or an F, it is usually a mixture of the results of test scores, homework assignments, projects, and reports, along with the teacher's subjective reactions.

Grades can be significant indicators of the part of the material the child is understanding and remembering. They can also point out a learning gap that needs to be filled. For example, if a child earns a low grade in seventh-grade math, the problem may be that he never really mastered his multiplication tables back in the third and fourth grades and needs help in strengthening some basic math skills. A low grade in English can be partially the result of poor reading skills or a comprehension problem that needs immediate attention. Some low marks are the result of disorganization or difficulty in following directions. Sudden falling grades in the case of a child who has been doing well may indicate burnout, emotional stress in school or at home, or physical problems. So we need to look at what is *behind* poor grades and what difficulties the child may be having.

Grades are important factors for acceptance into honor societies, for receiving an academic award in secondary school, for assuring entrance into certain limited-admission colleges and universities, or for obtaining scholarship funds. But, for all of their beneficial qualities, the plain truth is that good grades do not guarantee success in life.

Good grades are nice, but there is only a small amount of direct correlation between academic achievement and success in the real world. There are many people who received low marks in school or college and yet went on to be wonderfully successful in their careers and personal lives. There are some students who worked hard and never excelled scholastically, but who, because of their struggles and hardships, developed the persistence and character necessary for survival and success in daily life. Some of these were people who had behavior or adjustment problems in school and later turned around. Some were people who found the rigidity and "cookie-cutter approach" of school a hindrance to their inventive minds or creative bents. Some were late bloomers.

Recognizing that academic achievement is not all there is to life helps us keep grades in proper perspective. If your child has had problems in school or has just muddled along, never winning the "Student of the Month" award, take heart as you read the hall of fame that follows.

When Winston Churchill was a child, he had a stutter and a lisp. His teachers found him hardheaded, arrogant, and too active, and he occupied the lowest rank in the British school he attended. Louis Pasteur, who failed the entrance exams to medical school on his first attempt and was labeled a "plodder," was the first scientist to discover microbes and germs and developed the first vaccines.

Ray Kroc, founder and builder of McDonald's fast-food chain, was a school dropout, as were the Wright brothers and Samuel Langhorne Clemens (later known around the world as Mark Twain).

Creativity, a willingness to take risks, task commitment, perseverance, initiative, a burning desire, a consuming interest, or an overwhelming passion—many of these factors have a bigger stake in determining a person's success than certain letter grades on a report card.

That's why I encourage you not to look at grades as the primary indicator of your child's potential. Instead, focus on what really matters: What is she learning? Is she being challenged? Is she making enough progress to do the reading, work the mathematical problems, and handle the course material? Is she excited about and interested in any particular subject or hobby? Is there something she wants to know more about? Are her individual gifts and talents being discovered and developed? Is she *learning how to learn*? A key ingredient for staying motivated is for both parents and kids to maintain this healthy perspective.

the ownership issue

Recently a friend complained about how hard it was to motivate her eight- and ten-year-old kids to get out of bed for school each day. First she'd go into their bedroom and say, "Hey, time to get up!" Fifteen minutes later, she'd turn on the light, saying a little more loudly, "You're going to be late for school!" A few minutes later, she'd be shouting and they'd be shouting back. Many mornings she was late to work because her kids stayed in bed longer than they should. This routine went on day after day, and Mom became more and more stressed out about her kids being late for school.

The problem was that Mom had assumed the ownership of her children's getting out of bed. It was really their responsibility. I encouraged her to get both children an alarm clock, show them how to use it, and let them get themselves up in time to eat breakfast and leave for school. If they chose to stay in bed, they would have to deal with the consequences of tardiness at school. Before long, these kids were more motivated to get up.

The same principle applies to the ownership of grades. Whose grades are they anyway? Sometimes we get so wrapped up in wanting our kids to achieve that we take over responsibility for the grades or the assignment. For example, a parent may stay up half the night doing her son's science project or rewriting her daughter's essay. In that case, the parent, rather than the child, begins to "own" the grades. This situation inevitably leads to lowered motivation on the child's part because if the parent assumes responsibility for his performance, the youngster has less reason to try. He begins to think, *Why care? Why put out so much effort? Mom and Dad will take care of it.*

It helps to be supportive, encouraging, and genuinely interested when our child brings home his grades. We can boost motivation by taking an individual approach to reviewing our child's progress, not by getting the siblings together to compare results, but by sitting down and showing real parental care and concern. We can put the ball in our child's court by asking some good questions:

- "How do you feel about the grade (or grades) you received?"

- "What does this report card mean to you?"

- "Do you want to make any changes in how you are study-ing or organizing the material during the next term?" (Encourage your child to jot down the subject and one change to make for the term ahead.)

- "Is there any way your teacher or I can help you meet your study goals?"

If your child consistently receives a lower grade than she is capable of earning, do some troubleshooting. Consider your home environment and whether it's helping or hindering your child's learning. Consider the school environment, including the teaching methods used. The difficulty may be something as simple as the fact that the child sits next to a misbehaving student who con-stantly harasses and disturbs her. In some instances, the young-ster may not be able to see the chalkboard or hear the teacher. All these things can affect a child's performance.

motivating without pressure

Here are some tips on how to respond to grades without exerting undue pressure:

- *Avoid punishment.* Overreacting and applying punitive measures such as docking an allowance, grounding, and taking away favorite activities sets up a power struggle without producing any improvement in performance, says Dr. Arthur Bodin.[8] The child becomes determined to win the power struggle, which can drive him further away from his parents and squelch any desire he may have to improve his performance. Hasty or harsh punishment often causes a child to begin to hate school and the learning process and to resent his parents, which lowers his motivation even more. Children also get caught up in anxiety about the punishment, rather than focusing on their studies and what they need to be learning.

- *Avoid criticism.* Negative remarks such as, "I knew you'd mess up," or "In our family a C is the same thing as an F" tend to batter the child's already shaky self-worth and throw cold water on any motivation he might have to improve.

- *Consider scheduling a parent-teacher conference* to look for solutions, especially if the work seems too difficult for your child or you're puzzled about the cause of the child's poor showing and what to do about it.

- *Avoid paying for grades or offering bribes.* Some parents offer money, cars, clothes, and even vacation trips for a certain grade point average. But these material rewards tend to work against a child's success and diminish his chances of developing any real motivation for learning. When one sibling is paid for grades and another is not, rivalry and discord are increased in the family. (And besides, if you start this payment method when your kids are young, it's going to get really expensive by high school!)

Through years of teaching, I've found that the best students are generally not paid for grades. When a child is paid for his grades, he sees his work as something he did for the money rather than something he did because he loves knowledge, because learning is useful, or because he enjoys the activity. The more he is paid, the harder it is for the child to internalize the value of learning for its own sake.[9] I realize that many parents do pay for grades and that this is a controversial issue. I still suggest that if you use treats or money, it only be on a short-term basis. If we want to help our children develop any intrinsic motivation, we need to consider that research has shown if a child who naturally likes to do something is consistently rewarded or paid for doing it, he begins to work for the reward rather than for the enjoyment of the activity itself.

A child's good report card, achievement, or progress can be celebrated with praise, a surprise pizza, or an outing, just like you'd celebrate a sports victory or piano recital, but hopefully the child is also receiving praise and affirmation at times other than just report card week.

focus on learning

Instead of focusing on grades, we need to communicate to our children that learning itself is important and valuable. Because in the big picture, it's the learning that matters.

Dr. David Elkind, Tufts University psychologist, says,

> Too often parents get extremely caught up in the *grades,* and then they say to their child, "Why doesn't this motivate you?" Well, grades are not motivating really, but what is motivating is the whole process of learning and the excitement and challenge of that. Grades are kind of dull things to get excited about. By emphasizing grades, we may kill children's motivation. So what we should do is to talk with our children about what they are interested in, read to our children, take them to the museum, take nature walks, go to the zoo, see good films and stimulate their thinking. In our own reading, ask questions, provide a model of learning and curiosity, and then children can come to that naturally.[10]

We'll help motivate our kids if we shift our focus to the content of *what is being learned.* The important thing is not just that the child learns some facts, puts them down on an exam, and gets a mark for which he receives a stick of candy or a special treat if the grade is high enough. We want our children to discover how to learn, how to think, how to organize time, and the value of knowledge and hard work.

Edith Schaeffer, author of *What Is a Family?,* shared her wisdom on this topic with me:

What's important is that education is knowledge that *interrelates.* The more you know about history, then the more you understand about when medicine started. What you are learning interweaves with other subjects: art, music, literature. If a parent can supplement and interweave and make more interesting what is going on in the classroom, the child's education is greatly enriched and the child is more motivated.[11]

When we enhance our children's education this way and encourage them to pursue what they love to find out about, their motivation will grow and they'll have more courage to step out and into new learning situations—whether they are A students or C students. Most important, whatever their grades, our children need our unconditional love. When we let our children know that we love and accept them regardless of what grades they make, we help them cultivate motivation for all the difficult tasks in life.

PART 2

motivation boosters

motivation booster #1:
patience

One of the best things we can do for our kids is to have patience with them. Our patience is much more motivating than pushing or trying to force performance or maturity. Let's look at patience in three key areas: the preschool years, transitional times, and late bloomers.

patience with preschoolers

Sometimes as parents we expect too much emotional and mental maturity of preschoolers and early elementary-age children, especially those who are larger physically, have early verbal skills, and sound older. We may think the behavior of younger children is supposed to match that of their older siblings. But it helps to be patient with our younger sons and daughters, seeing them at the age and stage they really are—not "just like big brother," not like little adults—and not hurrying them to carry more responsibility or produce more achievements than they are able.

Dr. Louise Bates Ames gives us some sound advice on this point: "Respect individuality. Respect immaturity. Respect your child for what he or she is now, as a preschooler. There may never be a happier time."[1]

Being patient doesn't mean being passive or permissive. As parents, we love, discipline, teach, and correct. But knowing what is and what isn't normal behavior in preschoolers and children of different ages helps us avoid being too hard on ourselves or the child for her displays of childish irresponsibility or immaturity.[2]

"Knowing what is reasonable," adds Dr. Ames, "also means that though your hopes and goals will remain infinitely high, you will, hopefully, be able to wait." Waiting, she says, is a very active thing indeed. "It often takes a good deal of energy to restrain that impulse to push, shove, suggest, insist, and even punish for poor performance or lack of performance."[3]

Patience is a wonderful gift we can give our children that will help them to be enthusiastic and motivated as they learn and grow and as we relax and enjoy them right where they are.

not pushing preschoolers

We also need to look for early childhood programs that don't push our kids. When you're choosing a preschool, kindergarten, or early elementary school for your child, here are some things to look for:

- Is the environment warm, loving, and supportive?

- Do teachers seem to understand and genuinely enjoy the children?

- Are there opportunities for learning through exploration, experimentation, observation, building, dramatic play, and hands-on activities, instead of just pencil and paper activities such as worksheets?

- Are the children free to learn and develop at their own pace, or is there a rigid prereading and math program and emphasis on getting the "right" answer?

- Are there opportunities for children to be active and use their large motor skills in the learning process, or are they required to sit at desks and accomplish tasks appropriate for older children (those demanding a lot of close work dependent upon visual and fine motor skills)?

Let me encourage you to visit and observe any school (and classroom) in which you're considering placing your child. Don't base your decision on someone else's experience or your neighbor's opinion as to which program is best suited for your child. After your child has been enrolled for a few weeks, schedule a follow-up visit. See how well she's enjoying the program, progressing in her learning, and interacting with teachers and classmates.

Whether at school or home, young children need plenty of time for play. For young kids, *play is learning*. Playtime aids a child's growth. It embodies a high degree of motivation and achievement. It offers opportunities for the child to make decisions and solve problems. Play offers freedom of action and contains elements of adventure. Unfortunately, kids, even preschoolers and kindergarteners, seem to have less time for play these days and are participating in competitive team sports at younger ages. Dr. Ames notes that "play is the young child's world of sports."[4] When children climb, run, push, pull, and build, they develop their large muscles. They use their minds and stretch their imaginations by making up their own games. By manipulating small objects such as toy cars and puzzle pieces, they develop and improve their fine motor skills.

Young children learn by seeing, touching, and engaging their senses. They learn more about math by counting concrete objects such as beans or bears than by struggling with abstract symbols on paper. They learn to reason, solve problems, and cooperate with others by building a backyard fort. Blocks and paints, sand, dolls, cars and trucks, modeling clay—these are the materials of a young child's world of play and learning.

As kids grow, they get busier and have to hurry more and more. One mom told me, "We always said, 'Hurry up and finish eating. Stop playing. We've got to get to the next thing.'" Their hurrying escalated until both parents and kids were so cranky and stressed out that they were having sleeping problems. When they finally let their daughter drop an activity and have some time for free play, things got better.

When we give our kids so much stimulation without enough time to relax, it's like baking bread without giving it time to rise. During school, structured activities, and sports, their brains stay busy taking in lots of information. While they're resting, sleeping, or playing, their brains make the connections that are major parts of the learning process.[5] When they're constantly in a time crunch, rushing here and there, it actually impedes learning and motiva-tion. But a little downtime can boost motivation.

patience in transitions

Mrs. Roberts came in with a stack of her sixth-grade daughter's science papers and deposited them on the teacher's desk. "Why is Beth making a B? She's not a B student in science. She made all As in elementary school."

"Well," began Mrs. Roberts, "Beth seems to be doing pretty consistent B work in science, with the exception of two Cs on daily tests. She's still adjusting to being in middle school and having more responsibilities to keep up with. Her work in math has been average so far. But the area in which Beth really shines and shows great enthusiasm is reading and creative writing."

Beth's mom couldn't accept the fact that her daughter was no longer making all As. Frequently during the big change from ele-mentary school to middle school or junior high, children's grades in certain subjects will fall. Their marks in elementary subjects may have been all As because they were based primarily on effort, work habits, neatness, and completed assignments.

In middle school or junior high, however, where courses are departmentalized and students have a number of different teachers, kids may do very well in one subject and only average in another. It's hard to accept a mark of "average" or even "above average" on a middle school or junior high report card when your child made top scores in elementary school. Teachers in middle school and junior high also focus more on vocabulary learning and skill development in each subject. Reading, memorizing, and digesting printed material are given new importance, and children's individual abilities and interests begin to be more defined.

The change from middle school to high school also involves a shift in emphasis. In this transition, adolescence is well under way. The middle school environment was more nurturing, with greater explanation and teaching of basic skills. Now more critical thinking is called for. Class time shifts to more lecture presentation and group discussion. Students with strong visual skills who have excelled in the many visually oriented tasks of earlier years may experience a drop in grades if they haven't developed the good listening, note-taking, and verbal skills necessary for classroom participation. There is less spoon-feeding of facts.

"You're in high school now," teachers say. As one freshman student remarked, "In Physical Science, my instructor gave me a sheet with the first semester assignments, an outside reading list, and a test schedule. I felt like I was on my own." If your child has failed to develop any particular study skills along the way, this can be a hard time for him.

How can we help our children with these difficult transitions? We can be calm (which is not always easy!) and patient as our children learn the new skills required of them, find their footing, and make the adjustments needed to survive in the new middle school, junior high, or high school environment. What's the opposite of calm and patient? Excitable, irritable, anxious, angry, frustrated, hysterical, and hotheaded. We might automatically fall into one of these responses, but it will only make the situation worse. We can be encouraging if the results at the end of the first grading period are not what we or the child had hoped. We can avoid demanding that the child do perfectly in everything, understanding that he may do better in some classes than others. We can provide support by helping him stay organized and by keeping in touch with his teachers.

Patience with Late Bloomers

Patience is the art of hoping.

VAUVENARGUES[6]

One of my favorite children's books is *Leo the Late Bloomer* by Robert Kraus.[7] If your child tends to be a late bloomer in any area, this would be a good book to read aloud together. The main character, Leo the little lion, can't do anything right. He can't read. The wonderful illustration shows how sad Leo is about this situation as he sits in a tree, bewildered by the written page before him while all the other animals are happily reading. He can't write except for scribbling. He can't draw like the rest of the creatures of the forest. And he eats sloppily while all of his friends eat neatly, of course.

"What's the matter with Leo?" asks his father.

"Nothing," replies his mother. "Leo's just a late bloomer."

Better late than never, thinks Leo's father.

The rest of the story goes on to describe how every day and every night Leo's father watches him for signs of blooming. He watches and watches, and still Leo doesn't bloom.

Somewhat discouraged, Leo's father asks, "Are you sure Leo's a bloomer?"

"Patience," answers Leo's mother. "A watched bloomer doesn't bloom."

So the snow comes and then spring, and Leo's father is no longer watching. But Leo is having a fine time playing and exploring and growing!

"Then one day, in his own time," the author tells us, "Leo bloomed!"

We celebrate with Leo as he reads, writes, and draws with a flourish. He even eats neatly. And when Leo speaks, it isn't just a word; it's a whole sentence. The sentence is, "I made it!" On the last page we see Leo and his dad and mom hugging one another. We want to hug them too!

The message of this book is for both parents and children: We all need to have patience with late bloomers, to believe in them, and to know that, like Leo, in their own time *they will bloom.* They will learn, they will develop, they will become all that they can be.

Most children are late bloomers in some area. Some kids can tie their shoes at age four and others can't do it until they're seven. Some children ride their two-wheelers at age three while others still can't until they're six or seven. Some kids are slow starters in language skills. In whatever area our kids are late bloomers, we can have faith in their abilities and individuality, trusting their individual timetables of development. We can make sure that they have the support, nurture, and encouragement they need at home and at school while they are growing—*before* they start blooming. We wouldn't impatiently stamp our feet, insisting that our prize petunia bloom before it is ready. Neither does it help to demand that our children bloom prematurely.

Having patience with late bloomers is often not as easy as it sounds. It can frustrate parents to no end when their child appears to be behind all the other kids. A friend of mine tells the story of her first grader who had been trying to learn to ride a two-wheeler without much success. It seemed all the other kids on the block could ride their bikes with ease. This mom expressed her frustration to several other moms of first graders, and surprisingly, she found three others who were just as impatient with their kids' lack of bike-riding ability. Immediately after talking about it, these moms felt better and realized they needed to take a more patient approach. Additionally, they hit upon a plan to take the stress off these kids, who were undoubtedly aware of their parents' frustration: They arranged a weekend outing to a school playground with all the kids and their bikes. There, each mom worked with a child on his bike-riding skills—but not with her own kid. They found they were much more patient with someone else's child, and by the end of the afternoon, every one of those kids was riding his two-wheeler by himself.

Parents should also think of blooming in areas outside the box of academics and the three Rs. Some kids' success will emerge in discovering and developing their gifts in musical, artistic, technical, or athletic fields. One child may bloom as an actor or a dancer; another may bloom as a landscape designer, an Internet networking whiz, or a songwriter and musician.

Tim had a natural ability to figure things out. Although his degree of academic achievement was not like that of his sister's, his parents didn't put him down. They didn't compare or limit him because he didn't become an accountant like his dad or his big sister. Shortly after high school, Tim landed a job as an electrician and went on to earn his apprentice and journeyman's licenses. He gained confidence and skill as he continued to develop his natural mechanical abilities. Now he has an excellent career as the owner of an electrical services company.

Randy was one of six children and suffered from a speech impediment from birth until five years of age. He had problems in school and was not good in math, science, or English. But he started whittling at age four. Although he experienced frustration and rejection at school, some kindly next-door neighbors—an elderly couple—accepted him, spent time with him, and praised him for his unique woodcarving ability. Today Randy is a prominent Southwestern sculptor.

Broadening our definition of blooming paves the way for our children to develop their own talents according to their own timetables. The old saying may be true that the early bird gets the worm, but late bloomers can have great futures too.

Gary Decker is a good example. Gary began his education early at five years of age in a small school in Kansas. His older sister, always at the top of her class, was a hard act to follow. Gary did average work in elementary school and made Cs and an occasional D in high school. He was small for his age (only five feet three inches when he was a senior), so he had few opportunities to participate in sports. But his high school band teacher took an interest in him, so Gary concentrated on music.

During Gary's last year of high school, the school counselor said that she didn't think he was college material. His parents sent him to Wichita State University anyway, where he played in the marching band and majored in music. By now he was six feet tall.

Gary made average grades in college and earned a degree in music education. But after completing his college studies, he decided he didn't want a career in music, although he still had no clear direction for his life's work. For a time he served on a campus ministry. Later he got married and began working as an orderly in a hospital. There the chief general surgeon became his best friend and mentor. After training as an operating room technician for two years, Gary decided he wanted to be a doctor.

It took two more years of college to get all the science courses he needed to apply to medical school. During those two years of study, Gary made a perfect 4.0 grade point average, pulling up his overall average considerably. He was almost twenty-nine years old when he began his medical studies, which lasted four years. This classic late bloomer who didn't shine in elementary school, junior high, high school, or college became an excellent surgeon. Why was he able to go so far? Because it had been instilled in him that hard work, perseverance, and a willingness to delay gratification were essential ingredients for making something of himself. And because his parents and wife believed in him, patiently and lovingly supporting him in his efforts.

motivation booster #2:
storytelling

During a family reunion, my husband, our children, some cousins, and I sat around Uncle John as he related a favorite Fuller story, "John Matthias Goes to Dodge City." Children and adults listened, wide-eyed, as Uncle John told tales of the Old West:

My dad, John Matthias Fuller, went to Dodge City, Kansas, as a young man before the railroad lines were built because Dodge was having a boom—lots of jobs, money, and opportunity. John was a city slicker, a peaceful man who'd never hurt anybody. But because all the cowboys out there were wearing guns and he wanted to be in style, he went and bought a big six-shooter, belt, and holster.

One Sunday morning John wanted to show off his new accessories. He strapped on his big shiny six-shooter and swaggered down the street. Suddenly someone grabbed him by the collar and said, "Hand me that gun and gun belt." It was Bat Masterson, the famous marshall of Dodge City. He said, "Young man, you don't wear a gun in this man's town. You'll just be fodder for the guys who know how to use one. I'm going to take this gun and gun belt and keep them in my office and when you leave town, you can take them with you."

Well, Dad stayed there in Dodge City for three months, and then he decided to go back to Kansas City. Last thing he did was to go get his gun. There was a clerk in the marshall's office who said, "What'll you take for that gun?" The clerk had a roll of bills and bought the gun. That was the beginning and end of Dad's career as a cowboy.

Uncle John's tales put us right in the middle of the Old West, allowing us to imagine it in a personal way. The history books came alive as we pictured our own relatives riding horseback across the plains, helping to build the railroads, or staking a claim on the Cherokee Strip.

We all have a story to tell. Each family has a rich storehouse of tales: stories of faith and good character, true tales of overcoming adversity, stories that show the frailties and mistakes of ordinary people. Bible stories provide the histories of men and women in the larger community of faith—David, Sarah, Ruth, Peter. We have stories of our nation's history—the Boston Tea Party, the Revolutionary War, the Underground Railroad of the pre-Civil War era—and stories about our favorite historical characters, such as Clara Barton, Paul Revere, or Winston Churchill.

why is storytelling important?

A person without a story is a person with amnesia. A country without its story has ceased to exist.

WILLIAM J. BAUSCH

This is a book about raising motivated kids—so where does story-telling fit in? First, when we tell our children stories, it contributes to cultural literacy—a knowledge and understanding of the past and the present. Cultural literacy enables kids to:

- Read more fluently and with greater understanding

- Understand and appreciate the shared heritage, institutions, and values that draw people together as a nation

- Gain new knowledge and put it into perspective

Simply put, cultural literacy helps us feel we are a part of something bigger than ourselves. Being a part of a larger whole is very motivating. When we feel we're alone in the world, working only for ourselves, it's easy to get burned-out and wonder, *What's the purpose of it all?* But when we're living and working in the context of a larger story, we're more motivated to persevere—no matter what the task—because we have a sense of the importance of our own small role in the larger story.

C. S. Lewis, the famed writer and philosopher, suggested that in the heat of battle, he would have more faith in a group of soldiers who knew the stories of their country—tales of the great heroes and leaders—than in a group of soldiers who knew only their nation's constitution. He understood that those who knew the stories would have greater motivation to fight, to persevere, and to win because they knew they were a part of something larger than themselves.

Storytelling also has amazing motivational power when we are inspired by other people's journeys of overcoming obstacles, working hard, and obtaining rewards. I've seen kids' eyes light up when they hear amazing true accounts of people such as Helen Keller, Stephen Hawking, and Christopher Reeve, who overcame huge obstacles to accomplish their goals. Stories of heroes like Martin Luther King Jr. can motivate kids to stand up for what they believe. Michael Jordan's success encourages kids to work hard toward a dream. Tales of Grandma and Grandpa's voyage from the old country to start a new life in America can motivate kids to have courage and high aspirations.

The art of storytelling has largely been lost, and consequently many children don't know the history of their country or even their own family history.

put the story back in history

When the *story* is taken out of history, as it is when it's taught with a bland, textbook approach using facts and dates, it lacks life and fails to motivate learning. But when the focus is placed on major events, the people who lived them, and the literature of the era in which the action took place, kids learn and retain history much more readily. They are more motivated not only to learn, but to care about what they're learning.

One of my fondest memories of college life at Baylor University in Waco, Texas, is Mr. Reed's history class. On the walk from my dormitory to his class, my anticipation would begin to build. *What tale of adventure, war, conflict, or danger will Mr. Reed spin today?* I wondered. "Don't you want to spend the day sunbathing and watching soap operas with us instead of going to class?" my roommates tempted more than once as I grabbed my books. But I wouldn't think of missing that class. Listening to Mr. Reed was much more interesting than watching television or a movie. Unlike many college history professors, he didn't drone on from old lecture notes; he made the characters, countries, and cultures come alive as he dramatized the historical events of the day through vibrant, exciting storytelling. I was hooked on history. It became my second academic major because I didn't want to miss a single episode in the unfolding saga of Western Civilization and American History.

be a storytelling family

In chapter 2, we talked about the parent-child relationship as the first building block to motivation. Storytelling is a great way to build relationships and closer connections among parents, children, and extended family members. This direct interaction is especially needed in an age when parents and children spend much more time watching television than in family conversation.

You can help your kids know their past, pass on positive, enduring values to them, and boost their motivation for learning history through storytelling. In addition to this, storytelling provides incredible benefits for children's overall development: It instills good listening habits and develops concentration and a longer attention span. Storytelling ignites the imagination. The excitement of storytelling can make reading and learning fun and can instill in children a sense of wonder about life and learning. It's easy to make the connection: Kids are much more motivated to learn when they think of it as fun and exciting.[1]

Storytelling also has great value for its own sake—for the sheer delight that a well-told story can bring to a child. A story is a love gift from parent to child, grandparent to grandchild. Family stories give kids roots that are much needed in our society of blended families and transiency and convey a sense of security and belonging. They connect kids to the past and give them confidence to go forth into an uncertain future. As Vance Packard, an American writer, once said, "Knowing, in a deep-down sense, where you are from contributes not only to your sense of identity but to your sense of continuity."[2] We are much more motivated when we know not only where we came from but also where we're going.

Whether we gather around the family dinner table in the evening and tell stories of our day at school, work, or play or spend time together at a reunion relating bits of family history, through storytelling, we provide a means of passing on important life messages and creating precious memories.

This language practice at home is vital to kids' learning. The more proficient a child is in spoken language, the more successful she will be at reading written language. The child who is a good listener can retell stories and repeat and follow directions. Good kindergarten and first-grade listeners tend to become successful readers by the time they reach the third grade; good fifth-grade listeners do well on achievement tests in high school. Consistently, the most motivated kids tend to be those with solid language skills.

From the earliest years throughout childhood, literacy and learning depend a great deal on the amount and quality of language practice engaged in at home. These interpersonal skills enable the child to interact with teachers and other students at school and later with employers and other important people in the outside world.

spinning a yarn

An old storytelling song goes,

> *Where do stories come from, does anybody know?*
> *Where do stories come from, and where do stories go?*
> *Stories come from deep inside, then they travel far and wide.*
> *That's where stories come from, that's where stories go.*[3]

Where do *your* stories come from? Your family has tales of past generations as well as stories of your own era: accounts of the struggles and hardships of the first family members to settle in this country, memories of what life was like for grandparents and great-grandparents when they were young, recitations of father's or grandfather's experiences in the war, remembrances of your own childhood. There are also stories of your parents and their court-ship and marriage, as well as your own marital history: your first meeting, your first home, your first infant.

Kids love stories of their baby years and childhood. My own children never ceased to delight in hearing me tell about how Justin climbed on a worker's ladder to get on the roof at age two or when Alison took her very first airplane ride.

As a parent, you can tell favorite folk tales and original, made-up stories. Sometimes these stories grow out of moments parents and children spend together. My brother George always spun a bedtime tale for his boys—"The Adventures of Cowboy Bob." In their home hangs a painting of a cowboy on horseback, herding cattle across a wide prairie. One day his son Zack looked at the picture and asked, "Daddy, what's that?"

"That's Cowboy Bob and his famous horse, Paint," answered George. That night he told the first of many Cowboy Bob stories. Cowboy Bob rides across the plains, is chased by wild bush dogs and a herd of buffalo, leaps across canyons, and fords rivers. Cowboy Bob is a very active, adventurous cowpoke because his creator has an active, fertile imagination.

We don't hear many cowboy stories nowadays—kids are more likely to enjoy stories of space adventures, time travel, or aliens. But don't underestimate the power of these old-fashioned storytell-ing ideas. If your story is adventurous and imaginative with a bit of suspense or intrigue, your kids will love it.

Here are some valuable tips on storytelling:

- Use familiar story lines. Children love repetitive themes

and characters. My friend has two daughters who always want to hear the continuing adventures of the "Sister Princesses." Another friend, Kay, told the "Tales of the Mysterious Bear" every week when it was her turn to carpool. The first thing the kids asked when getting into the car was, "What happened next to the bear?"

- Put your child into the story. When I tell our granddaughter Caitlin stories about Mr. Squeeks (a mouse), Jake, and her other imaginary friends, Caitlin is always one of the characters.

- Start the story, and then let the child participate: "The mysterious bear came around the corner and was startled by a . . ." Stop and let the kids interject. They'll probably shout out something like "a tiger!" or "a kid!" Then you can continue your story based on what they say. This keeps you on your toes! The active participation in the narration of the story holds kids' attention and encourages their imagination.

- Tell personal anecdotes. Most children love to hear stories about when Dad and Mom were little. At Christmas they enjoy hearing about what toys Dad liked to get from Santa or what kind of dolls Mom used to play with. All kids like to hear stories of their parents' childhood milestones—when they lost their first tooth, what their first-grade teacher was like, how they handled their first fight with their best friend.

story starters

You don't need special training to tell stories to your kids or to get them involved in storytelling. Here are some springboards for stories:

- *Create instant tall tales* by having the kids name three unrelated objects, such as a koala bear, an apple core, and a candle or perhaps a giraffe, a haystack, and an Oreo cookie. Then make up a short three- or four-minute story using these objects in your narrative. You could also do it the opposite way—*you* name the three objects and have your child make up the story.

- *Round-robin tales* are good story starters. One person begins the tale, the next person in the circle adds some more action and perhaps a new character, and then the story line passes to the next participant. We enjoyed this game on long car trips.

- *Begin collecting hats* from garage sales, thrift shops, and Grandmother's attic. Hats stimulate dramatic play and serve as great story starters.

- *Hold a "family story hour"* after dinner once a month or when extended family gathers in which anyone, including parents, may share a story. Invite a grandparent, friend, or neighbor to come and spin a yarn, recount a memory, or describe an adventure.

For decades, librarians and folklorists have done us the great service of keeping the storytelling tradition alive and passing it on to future generations, but telling tales can be done at so many other times and places. Storytelling doesn't have to take place just at the local library. That's part of the joy of storytelling—it's spontaneous; it can be engaged in while washing dishes, raking leaves, riding in the car, or waiting in the dentist's office. Dinnertime is made even more enjoyable by an interesting account of the day's activities or by a rousing good tale. In our family, a car trip provided an occasion for my husband to tell the kids "Sinbad stories" to make the time go faster. And storytelling around a campfire is always a special treat. A starry night in summer is the perfect time to recount legends of the stars.

tips for storytellers

At a storytelling workshop for teachers held at Oklahoma State University, I learned that storytellers are made, not born. That news gave me hope, and I breathed a sigh of relief. *I can learn to be a storyteller,* I thought. I can recover the lost art of spinning a yarn, and so can you! Here are some things I learned that might help you become a better storyteller:

Learning a Prepared Story
To learn a prepared story:

1.   Choose a story you like. Read it over several times to make sure of your choice. Write it out in your own words and save it in a

special storytelling folder. If the story is too long, you may need to condense it.

2. Begin to get an idea of the basic text. You don't have to memorize the entire narrative. Outline the main events in sequence, noting the primary characters and important words. Review this outline mentally or on paper.

3. Try to picture the story by scenes.

4. Practice telling the story in your own words to the mirror or even to your pet.

5. Record the story on tape, video, or paper. If you're a word person, you might play back a copy of the story on tape a few times, perhaps while driving to work or doing some nonmental task. If you're more visual, you'll be aided by rereading the story or picturing it by scenes.

6. When you practice, add your own gestures, dialect, repeated phrases, and props (even a musical instrument), and use your own style to make the story yours.

7. Relax, be natural, and enjoy telling the story!

Generating a Personal History Story

To generate a personal history story, ask yourself or a family member these questions:

- Can you picture your childhood home? (Try to picture it just as it was in detail or even draw a simple house plan: the yard, the tree you played under, the house, the fireplace or dinner table where your family gathered.)

- What events happened there?

- Who lived there with you? Which visitors came most frequently?

- What was going on in the world at the time you lived there? (Who was president of the United States; was the nation at peace or at war; what was the economic and social climate like; which movies, songs, and radio or television programs were popular; who were your favorite entertainers; what were the current fashions like?)[4]

Thinking about these things usually generates many family stories.

Looking at old photo albums also often "primes the story pump." Children love to look at baby pictures of themselves, siblings, and parents, as well as photos of relatives. They are often fascinated by the stories and history that surround these family images:

- "This picture of Grandma and Granddad was taken when he came back from the war."

- "This is a picture of your father and me on our honeymoon at Turner Falls."

To tell a true story from your own experience, remember a specific age (when you were eight years old, for example) and then share about the time during that period when you were happiest, saddest, or most frightened. Relate the dialogue. Recall the sights, smells, tastes, sounds, and feelings of the experience. Was there some special insight or discovery you gained from it?

Interviewing Family Members for Stories

> *When an old man dies, a library burns to the ground.*
>
> OLD AFRICAN SAYING

You or your school-age child can also get some great stories by interviewing relatives when the family gathers for a reunion. Have a cassette recorder and extra tapes on hand. Some families even videotape interviews. Here are some questions to keep the stories rolling:

- Where were you born?

- Who were the first family members to settle in this country? Why did they come and where did they settle? Do you know any stories that conveyed what life was like for them or how they made their living?

- Can you tell me what life was like when you were growing up?

- Can you relate a story that was told to you as a child? What are some of your earliest memories? Adventures? Happy or sad times?

- What was school like for you? Did you have a favorite subject or teacher? Favorite games or pets?

- Who were your best friends and what did you do together?

- What beliefs or values do you think your parents tried to teach you to live by?

- Who influenced your life the most when you were growing up?

- What were your teenage years like? Courtship and marriage? Did you go to war?

- What have been the biggest problems, mistakes, or adversities in your life? How did you overcome them, and what did you learn from them?[5]

children as storytellers

Once when I taught storytelling skills to a classroom of kids, Tammy told me about her grandfather Maurice who during the Great Depression took a cow to college to pay for his expenses. Emily shared about her great-grandfather's mysterious forgotten sister. And Katie told of the time her mom accidentally drank kerosene and had to have her stomach pumped!

Parents and teachers who share their love of storytelling will find that their children are storytellers too. Your sixth grader may decide to dress up as Martha Washington and tell the story of her life as an oral project for social studies class. Perhaps you have shared with your child the times you took a big first step. Your child can also share his first big steps—memorable events, such as the first time he rode his bike without training wheels or the first night he spent at camp away from home.

Besides enjoying the fun of a story well told, children who learn to tell stories will develop confidence speaking in front of a group and learn to think on their feet. When your child tells stories, be an enthusiastic, interested listener because what's important is not only the joy of the story but also the warmth and closeness of the parent and child sharing it together.

motivation booster #3:
developing curiosity

"Who can tell me the name of this shape?" a kindergarten teacher asks, holding up a square block.

A flurry of hands wave in the air.

"I know!"

"Pick me!"

"Why do blocks have shapes?" one little boys asks.

"Clouds have shapes!" a girl in the back row adds.

If you walked down the hall and peeked into an eighth-grade classroom, what do you think you'd see? Attentive kids eagerly waving their hands and calling out answers? Not likely. Though kids are born curious and love to explore and learn new things, when they get older, their innate curiosity tends to wane. By the time they reach middle school, many students no longer see the classroom as an exciting, wondrous place.

Why the big change from the desire to know and discover during early childhood to the apathy many teens have regarding learning? The decrease is partly developmental. As Dr. David Elkind points out, preschoolers aren't bound by rules or conventions either in their thinking or their play. So they ask a myriad of questions in a free-thinking kind of way. By age six, kids operate out of a more logical hierarchy of thought. Their curiosity becomes more focused, thoughtful, and reflective. Teens are more focused on relationships and are more peer-conscious. Giving wrong answers causes them to "lose face." This fear of looking dumb can do much to stifle teens' inquisitiveness.[1]

But there are other curiosity busters. When kids' inquisitiveness is found annoying or unacceptable by parents or teachers, their curiosity wanes. If they're repeatedly told, "Do your worksheet, finish your homework, and don't ask questions" or "Don't bother me about all the whys of your science project; just do it and go watch TV," they begin to think it doesn't pay to be curious. Classrooms where teachers teach mostly through rote memorization and lectures or homes that are overly rigid and rule-oriented tend to stifle curiosity. If we always tell children what to think instead of giving them opportunities to discuss, debate, and explore, it will also dampen curiosity.[2]

Encouraging and nurturing kids' curiosity is one of the best ways to keep them motivated. If a kid is curious about how things work, she'll be motivated to pay attention in science class. If she's curious about how people lived in the past without electricity and running water, she'll be motivated to study history. Curiosity has a naturally motivating effect on all types of learning.

home: a place for curiosity

Asking why and really wanting to know the answer is a characteristic of a gifted, bright child who is inquisitive about things—from the nature of a tiny insect to how a car or computer works. And girls can be just as curious and interested in science as boys.

The good news is that home is the best place to grow this inquisitiveness. "New research on how kids develop curiosity and creative thinking reveals that the growth of intelligence comes from spontaneous emotional interaction with others—and interactions between parents and children are the most powerful and stimulating of all," says Dr. Stanley Greenspan, author of *The Growth of the Mind*.[3]

If encouraged and given opportunities for questioning and active exploration, all kids can remain inquisitive thinkers. The more curious children are, the more they'll learn and achieve academically. Curiosity is the desire for knowledge about something; it's an inquisitive interest or eagerness for information. Curiosity is a vital component of *intrinsic motivation,* the desire to learn something for inside, personal reasons or because something is fascinating. Picture the natural longing babies have to know about the world around them that leads them to explore with their hands, eyes, ears, and mouths or the desire a teen has to learn all he can about how to operate a video camera just because he's interested. In contrast, there is *extrinsic motivation,* the desire to do an activity or assignment for other rewards, such as good grades, prizes, or approval. Intrinsic motivation is a stronger influence on learning and its effect is long lasting or permanent, while extrinsic motivation wears off and is eventually no motivation at all.

Curiosity not only affects what kids learn but also fuels their sustained efforts. Curious students will keep trying hard to reach goals or get the desired information.[4] Curiosity is so linked to motivation that when curiosity dies, motivation and enthusiasm for learning wane as well. Because it's an ingredient that carries a child's learning far beyond the three Rs, we want to keep curiosity alive.

the role of parents

You play a big part in sustaining and encouraging your child's curiosity. As soon as kids are mobile, they investigate, experiment, and manipulate. Our one-year-old grandson Luke's favorite pastime was getting into things—whether it was Grandma's pots and pans or dirt in the garden. Toddlers watch and imitate, discover and dismantle because they have an inborn obsession to find out how and why things work.

By age three or four, kids are wondering about everything and asking thousands of questions:

- "Why is the sky blue?"

- "Why is the snow cold?"

- "Why does the cat have whiskers?"

By age five or six, most of them have developed basic attitudes not only about their world and the things in it, but more important about the learning process. Most of the time, these attitudes will have been shaped by adults' responses to their questions and exploration during their early, formative years.

What happens if we're annoyed by kids' questions and discourage their discovery? If Holly's curiosity is rejected when she reaches for a roly-poly on the sidewalk or wants to stop and watch a bird and ask why it can fly, if her parents are irritated by her exploration and inquisitiveness, she'll get the message that it's not safe to ask because it only gets her into trouble. "Don't touch that! Be quiet and come on!" When she's quiet, still, and passive, her parents approve and make her feel that she is a "good girl"; when she is inquisitive and curious about the world around her, she is a "bad girl." What is Holly being taught? *Not to learn.*

Dorothy Corkille Briggs tells us,

> *Questioning and experimentation with the unknown form the basis of advance in every field. Stamp out these qualities that are present in every normal newborn child to some degree, and you literally hold back progress for the human race. Every parent and teacher is responsible for keeping the lights of curiosity burning in children. Every child must know that it pays to wonder. He must think of himself because of his push to know.*[5]

On the road to knowledge, parental attitude can be a *stop* sign or a *go* sign that gives a child the "right of way" to keep traveling toward her destination.

handling questions

It's hard to always be attentive and encourage children's curiosity. But the overall pattern of how we handle their questions is what matters most. In some instances, as when pressed for time, your answer may be, "Mommy doesn't know, but maybe one of our books can tell us," or "That's a really interesting question; let's look it up on the Internet tonight or talk about it at dinner."

When you're handling children's questions, it helps to:

- *Give time to explain* what he already knows and what he wants to know about the subject. Try to discover what he's really thinking at his current level of reasoning. You can build on what your child already knows or jog his memory by saying, "Remember what we said last week when we talked about this question?"

- *Help your child think through the question* and deduce possible solutions. When seeing something that sparks her curiosity, she immediately seeks a ready-made answer from the nearest adult. She probably has an idea or a clue to the answer but just hasn't taken time to think it through. We don't have to give all the answers. We can help our child think through the question and guide her in discovering the answers. Sometimes kids come up with interesting theories and can formulate answers quite well.

- *Ask curious questions yourself.* When you go to the zoo together, ask questions such as, "Why do you think this animal has long legs? Is this animal a meat-eater or a grass-eater? Why is this animal's coat so thick and white? Which one of these animals is not like the others?"

It's great to encourage children's imaginations by asking questions about everyday things, for example, "What are all the ways we can use a toothpick?" They can wonder and think creatively about questions such as, "What can we do with this Styrofoam tray?" Perhaps they'll answer, "We can make an airplane out of it, or grow seeds in it, or . . ."

Middle school and high school students are sensitive to being made fun of for an off-the-wall answer or "stupid" question. So avoid putting them down for offering less-than-brilliant answers or asking a strange question. We can remember that there is no such thing as a stupid question—only ones that weren't carefully thought through. We can ask for teenagers' opinions and theories and be supportive when there's an interest or hobby they want to pursue. Reading science magazines and printing Internet articles on health, space, or environmental issues can also stimulate questions for our teenagers.

If we give children opportunities to inquire and explore and if we encourage their questioning, they will continue to observe, wonder, and make speculations and connections throughout life.

encouraging curiosity in your own backyard

Young children need places and times to explore because they learn through direct, firsthand experiences with the people and objects in the world around them. They need the safety of limits and supervision because their curiosity can lead them into danger. Using all of their senses, they develop security and confidence as they wonder, discover, and gain knowledge for themselves right in their own backyard or nearby park. This concrete learning is a vital foundation for future abstract, symbolic (pencil and paper) learning in books and school.

A variety of experiences indoors and out, at home and in the community spurs curiosity. Take your kids to the zoo, children's museum, or on a hike at a local nature center. Children also have fun at more unexpected places, such as an airport, a construction site, a bakery, a factory, a television station, or a lumberyard.

A magnifying glass also comes in handy for observing objects in more detail on outings. When you're near a flower garden, you can say, "Have you ever really looked inside a flower?" Then you can gasp a bit as you observe it with your magnifying glass. The child may want a chance to look and see what's inside that bud because of your interest. Then you can take one or two of the flowers (tulips work well), lay them out on a piece of dark paper, and give him a pair of scissors. He can cut the flowers and see the pollen that shows up clearly against the dark background. Together you can look at and identify the parts of the flower. In this way, your child gets to do a little basic botanical investigation and, best of all, his curiosity is aroused. You can also use the magnifying glass to more closely observe leaves, tree bark, skin, hair, fingernails, and objects around the house. Then, as certain things strike an interest in your child, you can find books or websites for more information.

Go on nature walks. You can check out the local bug population or collect rocks, leaves, or fossils. Keep a backpack ready for long explorations or short expeditions. In it, you can include:

- A magnifying glass

- An empty paper towel roll for observing (It can be cut in half for a more convenient size for smaller youngsters.)

- A "critter jar"—a glass or plastic container fitted with a mesh lid to let in air

- Old plastic tubs with snap tops for storing "treasures" found along the way

- A sturdy old spoon for digging

Have a nature scavenger hunt. For an interesting afternoon, try taking kids to a park, nature center, or forest and give each one a list of things to look for, such as five different kinds of leaves, three varieties of wildflowers, a pinecone, and four specimens of rocks.

If you're closer to a beach, engage in some hands-on ocean-ography exploration with a seaside scavenger hunt. When I went on a beach scavenger hunt with ten-year-old girls, I learned more about sea creatures in one day than I ever had in years of textbook science classes. Each person or team will need a small bucket or a plastic container with a snap top and a net or sieve. It helps to hunt at low tide and wear rubber boots or tennis shoes so you won't slip on the wet rocks. Hand out a list (use pictures for younger kids) of what to hunt for: sand dollars, hermit crabs, Irish moss and sea lettuce, different kinds of snails, sea urchins, slipper shells, blue mussels, crabs, clam shells, driftwood, starfish, seagull feathers, horseshoe crabs, and lobster tails or claws.

Encourage kids to collect things. Collections are a great way to encourage a love of science and the development of observation skills. Children can collect shells, leaves, insects, or anything that interests them. Some youngsters like to collect baseball cards, stamps, and spoons from different places. All they need is a shelf, drawer, or shoe box for display and storage. Organizing and arranging their collection lays the groundwork for the intellectual skills of classifying, categorizing, and evaluating.

everyday experiences and home projects

Chemistry sets, microscopes, and electronic sets are great, but you don't need special equipment to have curiosity-boosting experiences right in your own home. Here are some ideas to try:

- At bath time, ask your child to guess which bath toys will sink and which will float.

- Let your kids help you change the batteries in electronic toys and flashlights.

- Make or buy a birdhouse or feeder for the backyard and then watch and identify feathered friends when they are attracted to your bird habitat.

- "Adopt" a local tree. Your child can collect its leaves in each season; note seasonal changes in foliage, size, and color; and record in a logbook the different amounts of water the tree needs at various times of the year.

- If you're helping your child study the Civil War, don't just drill on dates and battles; debate the issues. Take different points of view on why battles were lost or won. Ask for his opinion.

- Set up a weather station in the backyard (your local library has good books that explain how) or encourage your child to observe the weather and record her observations on a homemade weather calendar. Each day have her note the various weather conditions. Put up an outdoor thermometer to check the temperature on a daily basis. Or when you're outdoors one evening just say, "Wow, look at that sunset! I wonder why it's more red tonight than last night" and let your child make her own observations.

in the kitchen

The old saying is especially true for the way kids learn: "I hear and I forget. I see and I remember. I *do* and I understand." Taking an active role when they're young will pay off. You can do all kinds of simple experiments in the kitchen that will help children develop the basic skills of asking questions, making observations, and drawing conclusions. When you're cooking, you can ask:

- Why does bread rise? (You can talk about the yeast growing.)

- Why should we be careful to wash our hands before we prepare food? (This is a good starter for a discussion of microbes and germs.)

- How can you tell from your bedroom that I'm fixing pizza?

Here are a few of my favorite curiosity-boosting experiments:

- *Bobbing Coffee Grounds:* Instead of throwing away your old coffee grounds, use them for an experiment. Take a teaspoonful and pour them into a glass of ginger ale. They will sink until they collect enough carbon dioxide from the carbonated water (the tiny bubbles are microscopic so they can't be seen with the naked eye). The coffee grounds will then float to the top of the glass, release their bubbles, and then sink again. If you get four hundred to five hundred coffee grounds bobbing up and down in a glass, your youngster will want to know, "Why is that happening, Mom?"

- *Colored Water and Oil Experiment:* Mix half a jar of colored water and half a jar of oil. Cap off the contents, and you'll have a miniature ocean in a bottle. The water, which is heavy, will sink to the bottom, while the lighter oil will float to the top. Tip the bottle back and forth and you will set off a wave action inside. You can ask the child, "Why don't the oil and water mix?"

- *Egg Mysteries:* To demonstrate buoyancy, fill two jars with a pint of tap water each. Add eight tablespoons of salt to one jar and mix. Then put an egg in each jar. Your child can watch as one sinks and one floats. If the child seems interested, you can ask him to speculate about why an egg will float in salt water but not in fresh water. You can talk about what makes the difference.

- *Balloon Fun:* Get a handful of different-sized and various-shaped balloons. Blow them up and let them go one at a time. Let your child make some observations: how far each goes, whether the flight was straight or erratic, how long each stayed in the air, and so on. You can ask, "Why didn't this big one go as far as the little one?" Next, have her tape a straw onto a balloon, blow the balloon up, run a string through the straw, stretch the string all the way across the room, and let the balloon go. Swish! The balloon will shoot across the room because it has a guidance system. (And she'll learn about mass and velocity.)

- *Bubble-Blowing Activity:* With bubbles you can demonstrate viscosity, that is, how the molecules stick together in the sphere. It takes about one-quarter cup of dish-washing liquid and three-quarters cup of water to make good bubbles. For longer lasting bubbles, add a teaspoon or two of glycerin. If your child gets his hands wet, he can hold the bubbles he blows; if he touches them with his dry hands, they will usually pop. Ask him why. With a pair of rubber gloves he can handle the bubbles and build them into pairs.

Showing your own interest is the best encouragement of all in these activities. In the same way, if you go to all this effort to encourage motivation, you don't want a rigid curriculum at school with little room for experimenting to diminish your child's curiosity. Find out what the school does to nurture kids' curiosity. If you're not satisfied, says Dr. Stanley Greenspan, take action:

> Band together with other concerned parents to ensure your children are exposed to a creative, stimulating learning environment. Sit in on a few classes. Take part in PTA to purchase hands-on science equipment. Meet with teachers and principals. With the support of enthusiastic, committed parents, kids can maintain their sense of wonder not only in the early years but throughout their lives.[6]

motivation booster #4:
learning about the world

We waited in the high school parking lot on a cold November evening in Maine with other families who, like us, would be hosting an international student for a week. Soon buses pulled in and young people from all over the world began filing off, excitedly looking for their host families. Jacq, a tall, blond, gregarious nineteen-year-old boy from Holland, quickly located us. We began a hectic but fascinating week as we shared family meals, swapped interesting stories, and got to know each other and our different cultures.

Jacq had brought many pictures of his family, his high school, his hometown, and other landmarks all over the Netherlands. He told us all about the educational system, the climate and economy, and everyday life in his country. Our kids were particularly interested in what a teenager's life was like in Holland.

Jacq, visiting America on a music tour, had lots of questions and observations about America based on his visits with families in other parts of the country. He even went to our daughter's sixth-grade class as a guest and shared with the students his experiences growing up as a Dutch boy in his native land. After his week at our house, Jacq wrote a gracious note of thanks, but we felt that we were the ones who had benefited the most from his visit.

Getting to know Jacq was such a positive experience that we decided to invite an international student from the University of Southern Maine to spend Christmas weekend with us. Zhu Hong, a petite, dark-haired young woman from Shanghai, was a bright freshman economics major. Although she had been in America for over a semester, she had not yet been in an American home. Having grown up in Communist China, she was eager to celebrate her first Christmas. Besides having the joy of sharing our traditions with someone who had never even sung a Christmas carol, we watched a full-length video of life in Shanghai and Beijing that Zhu Hong had filmed and narrated before leaving her homeland. We saw interesting images of the inside of university dorms, bustling city streets crowded with bicycles, and even a college dance. We learned things about the Far East we had never known before. Zhu Hong also gave us gifts from China as a bond of friendship.

Learning about people and cultures from around the world in this personal way is fascinating to kids and one of the most powerful motivators I've encountered. I watched my children's interest in the world around them grow as they became excited to find out more about other cultures. Bringing foreign students into your home is one of the most inspiring ways to teach your kids about the world.

international students in the U.S.

In any given year, several hundred thousand young people from more than 175 countries are in the United States to pursue undergraduate or graduate studies. They are among the most intelligent and promising youngsters in their native countries and will return as leaders. Zhu Hong, for example, was one of the top eighty students in Shanghai, a city of millions. These gifted young people come to America not only to study in our colleges and universities, but also to learn about our people, customs, and way of life. They learn best from visits with a family rather than remaining isolated in a dormitory with other international students.

As Rie Honjo, a Japanese student, said in a letter she wrote before she arrived for a scheduled visit at our house, "I am eager to be a member of your family for five days. And I want to learn various things about Oklahoma and learn better English speaking. So please help me." Many of these international students never get to see the inside of an American home. Instead, they spend lonely holidays without friends or family in nearly deserted dormitories far from home.

building bridges

Hosting a guest from another country has tremendous benefits, not only for you and your children but also for your guest. We can make a great difference in the experience of international students in America. We can build bridges of friendship. Whether our visitor has been from Taiwan, Japan, Holland, or China, we have found that the blessing of hosting foreign friends is a two-way street. We all learn together, and our children's motivation for learning about the world, geography, and the culture of other nations is boosted.

In this family adventure, you and your child will not only learn more about the international guest personally, but will also benefit from a greater knowledge of and appreciation for the customs, education, climate, attitudes, and way of life in her homeland.

Kelly Hagan, nineteen, is a member of a family who hosted many international visitors through the years. She was also an exchange student in Japan. "When our Japanese visitors were here and we took them to the Cowboy Hall of Fame," she notes, "we looked at things so differently; we noticed things we had taken for granted. We looked at the Fourth of July parade through their eyes, and afterward they showed us pictures of their Japanese festival days, parades, traditional dances, and kimono dress."[1]

Kelly's parents had lived in England for six years. Upon their return to America they found that they missed the contact with other cultures. So they began hosting international students and adults. As they opened their home and hearts to foreign guests, the Hagan family developed many long-term friendships with people from France, Russia, Mexico, Holland, Japan, and England.

Having international friends through their growing-up years also motivated Kelly and her brother Kevin to study foreign languages. Kelly converses readily in French and Japanese, and Kevin speaks French and Spanish.

reaching out

By visiting in a home, the international student has an opportunity for friendship and involvement with an American family. For the student just arriving from abroad, a host family is a great help in getting over the initial culture shock. She has someone to help ease the difficult transition and to interpret some of the different things encountered in a new and often bewildering environment. Most of all, a relationship with a host family serves as an antidote for the homesickness and loneliness the student often feels thousands of miles from home in a strange land.

"Thanks for your kindness and everything you did," wrote Kiyori, an international student from Japan who visited us. "I lived with you for only five days, but I had happy life with you. Especially I liked Fourth of July picnic, parade and choir concert. In Oklahoma City the people were very friendly and kind."

What Kiyori and Rie wanted most was to learn to speak more conversational English. That was difficult because although they had studied English for seven years in school, they could speak and understand little of our language. Our idioms were particularly difficult for them to grasp. They had a better command of written English.

We found music to be the key to helping them learn more spoken English. After dinner one night, I got out my guitar, wrote down the words for them to follow, and taught them some traditional American folk songs, such as "You Are My Sunshine," "I've Been Working on the Railroad," and "Row, Row, Row Your Boat."

We recorded our song session because they wanted to be able to practice when they returned to Japan.

Kiyori and Rie showed us photographs of their families, schools, and friends, as well as pictures of Tokyo and Hiroshima, Shinto shrines and temples, and the mountains of Japan. We learned about the typical Japanese diet. Our gentle, gracious Oriental friends taught us some Japanese words and songs and refreshed our lives during their stay.

Kiyori and Rie introduced our daughter to origami, the Japanese paper-folding art, by leaving delicate orange and red paper cranes and rabbits on her pillow. In addition, they left behind several packages of the brightly colored origami paper. Soon afterward, we found a book with diagrams showing how to do origami, which became a summer hobby for Alison.

getting in touch

To find a student, call the international student office or foreign student adviser on the college or university campus nearest you or contact Youth for Understanding, American Field Service, or your local chamber of commerce.

You can host international students in your home on a short-term basis for a designated period—a holiday, weekend, or week. There are also long-term arrangements in which the student doesn't actually live in your home but is assigned to you for a school term. You act as host family in the community providing ongoing care and friendship for the student.

smoothing cross-cultural exchanges

A smoother cross-cultural exchange will be established and maintained if you follow these simple suggestions:[2]

- Talk with your new foreign friend but avoid the common practice of raising your voice to make yourself understood. If he doesn't understand, repeat what you are trying to say in simpler, more formal English, using fewer slang words and fewer idiomatic expressions (such as "run to the store," "grab a bite of lunch," or "hop a plane"). Although effective oral communication may be difficult at first, don't be afraid to try it. Be patient and kind; try to put yourself in your international guest's shoes and imagine how you would feel trying to understand a totally foreign culture and language.

- Telephone in advance when you invite the student to share a meal or some family activity in order to give her plenty of time to arrange transportation and fit the event into her schedule of classes, study, and work.

- Show an interest in your student by encouraging him to talk about himself—his family, customs, education, home life, religion, ambitions, hopes, and plans. He may have pictures or maps he would like to show if you ask. He'll appreciate your listening.

- Ask her to teach you a greeting, a song, or other words in her language. Then teach her an American song.

- Ask what he would like to see or do in your community.

- If possible, let her bring a friend for dinner or get together with another host family and their international guest.

- Include the student in Thanksgiving, Christmas, and other holiday celebrations.

- After you've gotten to know each other better, ask your international friend if he would like to come to your home and prepare a traditional meal from his country.

- Don't feel that you always have to entertain your visitor. She may enjoy just taking part in regular family activities, including doing chores, helping prepare meals, and spending time reading, studying, or writing letters.

- If problems arise, consult the foreign student advisor on campus.

- If possible, read about your guest's home country. The knowledge you gain will increase the value and enjoyment of your shared experience. A website about the country, an encyclopedia, and other books from the library can provide lots of background facts and data.

children as hosts

Children make great hosts and hostesses for international students. With their natural curiosity, enthusiasm, and lack of inhibitions, they can help overcome cultural barriers and build bridges of understanding. Their spontaneity and lack of self-consciousness make a visitor feel at ease.

Alison, our youngest, was the most outgoing of the family in the presence of our international guests. Having only brothers, she was delighted to have two new college-age Japanese "sisters" sharing her room for a week. Although at first they could communicate very little in words, Alison accompanied our Japanese guests on an afternoon visit to a local shopping mall and discovered a favorite universal pastime shared by girls of all ages and nationalities: shopping. She also took our guests bike riding, swimming, and to an amusement park.

motivating children to learn about the world

Learning about the world doesn't have to be merely a school activity. In fact, children of all ages are much more motivated to learn the location of countries, states, oceans, and rivers if they see a reason to do so—because their family has an interest in people and cultures in other parts of the world, because they know someone from another country, or because they have read about other nationalities. Then social studies or geography is no longer just a bunch of meaningless, unconnected facts that they have to learn by rote.

Give kids a variety of experiences. My friend Carol and her daughters toured Washington, D.C., explored the NASA Space Station in Houston, went to Israel, volunteered in an inner-city school together, worked on an Indian reservation, and did mission work in Guatemala. Each girl went with their dad on "Take Your Daughter to Work" day and learned about the business world.

Here are some other ways to motivate your kids to learn about the world:

- Place a large world map on the wall in the family room, the playroom, or your child's bedroom. Maps are a valuable resource in geographic study. If there's a big event on the news, you can easily call the incident to the child's attention and say, "Let's see where that took place; can you find it?" If there is severe weather in some part of the country or world or if an important environmental issue is in the newspaper, you and your child can look together to see where it is taking place. If your child is studying a particular country in social studies, you can ask her to point it out to you on the map.

- Use thumbtacks to attach to a map the name or picture of relatives or friends who are visiting, moving to, or living in different parts of the United States or world.

- Use laminated maps so you can write on them or plot the route of a trip with a washable marker and then later erase it. In one family we know, the dad plotted his routes when he went on business trips and the mom marked her overseas medical mission trips so their children would gain a sense of where their parents were and develop an interest in the world. Before the family went on a trip, they plotted their route together on the map with an erasable highlighter.

- Let your kids browse the Internet's many resources to learn about the world. One of the largest free reference sites is www.factmonster.com, which contains a profile of every country in the world with information on its history, land, government, flag, religion, and people. It includes a section on national holidays around the world, games, and much more.

- Watch travel programs on TV.

- Buy soft, stuffed globes in bright colors that your younger child can play with or use as pillows.

- Help your child find an e-mail pal in another country, perhaps the child of missionaries or military parents. Nothing beats person-to-person correspondence for kids who want to learn about the world. With the quick response time of e-mail, a real friendship can develop. Check with the League of Friendship if you don't have friends overseas. They can be contacted at P.O. Box 509, Mt. Vernon, OH 43050, or 614-392-3166.

- Equip your child's room with wooden and cardboard puzzles of the United States and other countries of the world. Manipulating a piece and talking about the place it represents and the products that come from that area (which may be indicated on the individual pieces) makes learning geography both painless and enjoyable.

- Play games that help kids learn about the world, such as the popular "Trip Around the World," "Where in the World?" "World Traveler," or the electronic game "Geo Safari," which can be found at learning resource stores.

- Make different ethnic foods, take your children to an ethnic restaurant, or treat your kids to ethnic snacks at a folk festival. While you eat, talk about why people of different cultures eat different foods. For example, why do the Japanese eat so much seafood? If your children look for Japan on a map, they'll realize it's a country of many islands.

- If you have friends who are from other countries or have lived abroad, invite them over to talk with your kids, share pictures, and discuss their language, work, and travels.

- Read books that describe journeys and stories from or about other countries. Many kids' books provide colorful images of different places and a sense of what it would be like to live in them. Drawings or photographs of distant places or situations can motivate kids to learn about other lands. *Chinese Children Next Door* by Pearl Buck, *Bell for Ursli* by Selina Chonz, and *Josephine's Imagination: A Tale of Haiti* by Arnold Dobrin are examples of books with descriptions of places that have motivated kids to love learning about other countries and people. There are scores of books about other countries at the library.

- Encourage your children to read magazines, such as *World,* published by the National Geographic Society, and *Discover,* published by Family Media, Inc. These can be found in schools and public libraries and have fascinating stories and articles for kids.

During holidays, discover with your kids how children in other countries celebrate. Holidays are great opportunities to learn about the customs of people around the world. Library books and the Internet are good sources for information on other countries' holidays.

As you show an interest in other nations and nationalities and keep abreast of world events and international affairs, your child will grow up with a wider knowledge of the world and a greater awareness and appreciation of different cultures.

motivation booster #5:
the attitudes of responsibility
and optimism

Did you know that by the time your kids are ready to receive their "wings" when they leave home for college or beyond, they've spent 32,234 hours under your training and nurture? Compare that to the mere 2,100 hours of classroom time it takes to earn a college degree. You have sixteen times more teaching and training hours with your kids than all the time they spend with professors in an entire university education.[1]

Sure, a lot of that time is spent eating, sleeping, practicing sports, and playing in the neighborhood. But you also have time within your child's growing-up years to teach her responsibility. It's a great skill that can help her be more motivated in school and in life in general. If we give our kids too much too soon, do everything for them, and expect little in return, they tend to turn out unmotivated. In my years in the education profession, I've heard lots of teachers say, "I can't motivate these students because their parents don't require anything from them at home."

One of the main ways I've found to teach responsibility at

home is through requiring regular chores. Maybe you've heard, "But Mom, I don't wanna!" We've all heard it. But if we want our kids to be motivated, they're going to have to take on household responsibility. Kids who have chores at home and develop a sense of responsibility tend to be better students. They have more confidence and more coping skills. If they become responsible, they'll be more successful in jobs, in their careers, and even in their own marriages and families. The events and daily happenings of family life offer lots of opportunities to help kids grow in responsibility.

life's little lessons

I'm all for children having lots of fun and play. But developing a sense of responsibility can start as early as the preschool years as you encourage your three-year-old to help you in little ways in the kitchen and teach him simple household chores. Little kids feel big when they get to help Dad prepare a Saturday breakfast or help Mom clear snow off the front porch.

One of the secrets is recognizing age-appropriate ways kids can help. That way we don't overload them with chores but give them doable tasks. A two-year-old can pick up his toys and begin to make his bed with Mom's assistance. But washing dishes and taking out garbage wouldn't fit a two-year-old's abilities.

Six-year-olds can feed the dog, pick up playthings, take their dishes to the kitchen, and put dirty clothes in a hamper. Older kids can set the table, empty wastebaskets, load and unload dishes in the dishwasher, and eventually help with yard work.

Charts work well for some families in fostering follow-through, and to-do lists are effective with older kids. Many children feel a sense of accomplishment when they can cross off each item on their daily list of chores. Even prereaders can follow instructions on a daily chart when pictures are used to indicate the tasks.

When children say, "I can't do that," they may mean, "I don't know how." You can use a patient, step-by-step approach to demonstrate a new task and to allow practice. Some kids like to work independently, and others want a show-and-tell approach—working alongside parents until they feel competent doing the chore. Avoid remaking the bed or rewashing the dishes under your child's gaze, however, or he'll feel as if he's not good enough.

Help him persevere, no matter what the task, and your child will learn the stick-to-it commitment and determination that will keep him from throwing in the towel even when a situation or job is challenging or downright hard. Your child may be super smart, but without exercising the steady perseverance and persistence it takes to overcome obstacles, he won't accomplish much in the real world or learn much of anything.

Finally, give lots of positive feedback, even if the task isn't done perfectly. If you focus on the effort your child has put in, you'll build his motivation for helping and thus his sense of responsibility.

building optimism

Nine-year-old Meghan started having trouble in math class when the teacher presented long division problems. One night her mom saw her struggling with her homework. "I'll just never get this! I'm terrible at math!" Meghan moaned.

As much as her mother tried to help, Meghan was convinced she couldn't figure out the problems, so she finally threw her book down, gave up, and went to bed. Have any of your kids ever felt so frustrated they wanted to quit? Or developed a negative attitude about a sport, a certain subject, or your church? Researchers are finding that one of the keys to learning and motivation is an optimistic attitude.[2]

Optimism enables a kid to overcome failure, keep trying, and develop a plan of action. While some people seem to be inherently more optimistic than others, optimism can be learned. Even kids who tend to be negative, pessimistic thinkers can develop a more positive view of life and their own abilities.

How can you teach your child optimism? Start by helping her see that useful information, such as what doesn't work or what to try next, can be gained by mistakes. The next time your child is down in the dumps about a mistake, share the stories of scientists who failed their way to success, such as Thomas Edison who flubbed thousands of experiments before he developed the light-bulb or Jonas Salk who endured many failed attempts before he discovered the right polio vaccine that stopped a tragic worldwide epidemic. Thomas Edison said, "I was always afraid of things that worked the first time."[3]

Read stories to your kids about people who kept trying in spite of obstacles and failures so they can see that if at first they don't succeed, they're in good company. Michael Jordan, for example, failed countless times to make a crucial shot in a game, yet he's one of the all-time greatest basketball players in America.

Even great leaders have failed. Dwight Eisenhower, the thirty-fourth president of the United States, was rejected three times for command positions in the military before he was appointed Supreme Commander in 1942. Harry Truman, our thirty-third president, failed in business and went bankrupt at age thirty-seven. He worked for fifteen years to pay off the debt. Abraham Lincoln faced tragedies and was defeated several times in congressional elections but later became the sixteenth president of the United States. Be on the lookout for other historical or modern-day people who have come back from setbacks and triumphed against all odds. As you share these stories and model a "comeback" instead of a "give up" attitude, you'll be helping your child grow more optimistic whether he's trying to learn to play an instrument or tackle a new sport or skill.

Kids need to know that failure is only temporary. As Winston Churchill, prime minister of England during World War II, said, "Success is never final. Failure is seldom fatal. It's courage that counts."[4] That's worth passing on to our kids. It will especially help those who think pessimistically about their failure on a test: "I'm going to flunk the whole course. I probably won't even pass seventh grade." Thinking negatively about their chances on the next challenge or test isn't productive. A pessimistic outlook only causes kids to put forth less effort, and their performance spirals downward.

Feeling sad for a short time is normal, but instead of allowing your child to dwell on the worst scenario that could happen or have thoughts about what a loser she is, help her see that using a different way of studying can help overcome the failure. For example, she could start studying a few days before the exam instead of trying to cram everything in the night before. Encourage your child to avoid attributing everything to bad luck or blaming other people (She might say, "It's my teacher's fault" or "My small group did a lousy job on that project.") but to own up to her part. Remind her that hard work will make a difference.

You can also stir up optimism by reminding your child of some areas in which he has done well or succeeded. (We tend to forget these when we're faced with discouragement or failure.) Recalling the little victories and realizing how far he's come builds courage to try again. With your support, he'll become more motivated—no matter what challenges he faces.

PART 3

motivation busters

motivation buster #1: perfectionism

Even as a small child, Sarah was a perfectionist. If she spilled a little ketchup on her dress, she fell apart. If a friend left something out of order in her room, she became upset. In school, she was hesitant about reading aloud or writing down words for fear she might make a mistake. In the third grade, receiving an A- on a paper caused her to cry for an hour. She became disturbed if her papers weren't neat enough.

The key to recognizing whether a child has a problem in this area is to notice if she is consistently worried and anxious about perfection. If, in her estimation, a school paper is either perfect or worthless, if a musical piece must be played exactly or not at all, if she must be the best at whatever she does because she fears that otherwise no one (not even her parents) will like her, perfectionism may be becoming a problem.

Our world applauds perfection, and wherever kids look, they're told perfection is the goal. Many high-ability children (especially those of perfectionist parents, whose house is always immaculate or who tell their kids to recite their Bible verses perfectly) become prisoners of their own expectations. They become excessively driven and, more than anything else, fear making a mistake. When the drive for excellence and being the best turns into a compulsive drive for perfection, trouble follows.

This is particularly true in regard to kids and their motivation to learn. A counselor I know once said, "Walking a tightrope over Niagara Falls is stressful. One misstep and you're history. That's life as usual for a perfectionist child." In the minds of perfectionist children, imperfection means failure. Their need for perfection can lead them to avoid challenges and give up too easily. They may become defensive about what they don't know. They may develop a tendency to focus on past failures and attribute them to low ability. Sometimes they make excuses and don't turn in assignments, often becoming underachievers even though they're smart. If they can't be the best, they won't try at all. After all, if they don't finish the assignment, no one can tell them they didn't do it right![1] In addition, when these kids do achieve, they often don't derive any joy or satisfaction from their success because they are always looking down the road to the next goal or challenge.

countering perfectionism

Perfectionism doesn't just affect kids' performance in school. When they excessively push themselves, it can cause physical and emotional problems as well. Dr. Sylvia Rimm, who has studied perfectionism in kids, suggests that parents need to take "perfect" out of their vocabularies.[2]

In addition, there are other steps we as parents can take to counter the pitfalls of perfectionism:

- Help your child put success and failure in proper perspective by letting him hear you admit your own less-than-perfect actions without perceiving them as major catastrophes. You could share a story of the time you made a low grade on a test or failed to make the team or point out that though you blew it on a project, you figured out a different way to make it work. This kind of open dialogue about personal imperfection and failure helps children realize and understand that other people, even adults, make mistakes yet still go on leading happy and productive lives.

- Help your child approach new experiences with an understanding that mistakes are a natural part of the process of learning, life, and growth. Perfectionists often avoid new experiences because of a fear of failure. They won't try anything new because they hate making mistakes. Encourage your child to go into new situations with an attitude of, "I'm learning this. I don't know anything about it yet, so I give myself permission to make mistakes while I'm learning."

  You can help your child keep her focus on the *learning* aspect of the new activity or skill rather than on the *achievement* aspect. "I've stopped striving for perfection in everything and started striving for excellence," says one recovering perfectionist teenager.

- Realize that perfectionism often shows up as procrastination, especially in school-age children. When a child consistently delays starting a project or writing an essay, it may be because he wants to produce perfect work and feels overwhelmed by the enormity and complexity of the task set before him; therefore, he doesn't want to even begin it. If this is the problem, help him break the assignment or task into smaller, manageable steps or chunks, such as dividing the term paper into three parts and marking the completion of each step with high fives, affirmation, or something to celebrate his progress.

    A friend of mine is forty years old, yet she'll never forget the fourth-grade assignment in which the students were given a month to turn in a report on California's twenty-one missions. Up until then she'd been a stellar student, never faltering. Her parents and teacher were shocked when the due date came around and not only had she failed to finish her report—she had never even started it. A classic case of perfectionist paralysis had set in, and she hadn't had the courage to ask for help.

- Avoid offering profuse, overdone praise for everything—words such as *brilliant, genius,* and *prodigy* that put children under pressure to be perfect. While praise is positive and needed by children in recognition of the steps they have completed or the accomplishments they have achieved, extravagant praise can produce a fear of failure and aggravate perfectionism.

Praise needs to be given not just for what a child *does,* but also for who she *is.* Children need to know that they are appreciated for who they are, not just for what they accomplish or achieve. They need to be praised for actions and attitudes that have nothing to do with their ability or talent, such as sharing a toy or prized possession, making a get-well card for a sick friend, displaying compassion for someone less fortunate or less gifted, sweeping an elderly person's porch, or caring for the family pet. Word pictures can help describe the good qualities that a parent desires to see manifested in his child. For example, my friend Joanna praised her five-year-old daughter Rachel for tending to her puppy and kitten: "You're just like a mother bird with her baby, Rachel; you take such good care of Hugo and Kitty."

- Avoid stirring up competition among your kids in the family or in the classroom. Perfectionists tend to be highly competitive anyway, and comparisons only serve to heighten their natural rivalry. Negative comparisons of children to siblings or friends lower their self-esteem and increase their fears about not measuring up to parental expectations. When you affirm each child's worth without making comparisons between him and others, he grows in confidence. Instead of saying, "You've got to work harder than your brothers and sisters because you're so much smarter than they are," or "Why can't you do your homework as quickly as Jared does?" try to encourage the child to do his best for his own enjoyment and in his own time.

- Arrange to have your child engage in some activities outside of school that are relaxing and not tied to competition or winning. Encourage her to pursue her own interests and develop a creative outlet that is not graded—one that is done just for fun and enjoyment. It could be learning a musical instrument, hiking, scrapbooking, playing golf, jogging, skateboarding, or painting—anything positive that the child enjoys doing.

- Encourage and cultivate a sense of humor—in yourself and in your child. Humor can help overcome perfectionism and relieve stress. We all get uptight sometimes, but when we're able to laugh at ourselves, it decreases tension. It allows us to chuckle at our own mistakes and avoid becoming overly serious about every event of life.

- Help your child choose one or a few areas in which he would like to work toward excellence, rather than trying to be number one in everything he does. Sometimes we expect a gifted or talented child to be valedictorian of his class, student council president, the most popular student in school, and the best basketball or softball player. When we encourage kids to aim at excelling in a few important areas—those that matter most to them or those in which they have the most strength, ability, or interest—they can relax a little more.

the value of encouragement

What do we do when we are disappointed in our child's performance? How do we motivate her to do better? Children who are unmotivated usually have parents who use negative techniques to elicit performance, such as frowning at the child and expressing displeasure at what she is doing or failing to do. Often they get upset at every mistake the child makes. They criticize, withholding their praise or encouragement until the youngster has made some major accomplishment worthy of recognition and reward. This just makes perfectionist kids go into overdrive, and it isn't helpful for children in general. "As much as we know, the negative approach doesn't work," says Dr. Carol Kelly. "It's amazing how often parents resort to it when upset with their children's performance."[3]

In contrast, she says, there are lots of studies that indicate the power of encouragement—studies that prove that children who are motivated, achieve, and keep trying usually are the offspring of parents or guardians who act like cheerleaders. Instead of being demanding, they encourage their kids with smiles and hugs and applaud their efforts appropriately. If a child is unsuccessful in some undertaking, they don't make a big deal out of it. They talk about the situation or may laugh together about it. The child is encouraged to try again—like the Olympic ice skater who falls down, gets right back up, and goes on as if nothing has happened.

Such encouraging parents share in their child's excitement. They cheer *efforts* as opposed to only *ability*. They help him break tasks down into small steps. They don't wait until their child has learned to play the piano well enough to appear at Carnegie Hall before they offer praise; instead, they celebrate the steps along the way to eventual success. This kind of step-by-step approach makes things much more doable for the child. "Children have to learn that success comes from hard work, and that it takes time," says Dr. Kelly. "That is why they need lots of encouragement along the way."[4]

With parents' encouragement, kids who've struggled with perfectionism can enjoy going for their personal best instead of being *the best* in everything. Caleb had always avoided doing anything he wasn't sure he could do well. When he was counseled several years ago about his excessive drive for perfection, his parents were advised to get him involved in things he wouldn't be the best at. So they encouraged him to take piano lessons and play sports. He took piano lessons for a while, but it wasn't his passion. He didn't excel at sports, but even though he wasn't the star of the team, he found he really enjoyed playing sports and being with the other guys, and it helped him have a better outlook on life.[5]

motivation buster #2:
attention problems

"On your mark, get set, go!" we would call out before a childhood race.

Kids who are ready for learning begin by focusing their attention. But a major roadblock to learning for many children is a lack of attention skills. The child who has great difficulty focusing and concentrating on a task is at a disadvantage in the classroom and often loses motivation for learning.

Luke was enthusiastic and ready to learn when he began school. He was one of the youngest students in the class, yet bright and capable. By the time he reached second grade, however, his mother was getting weekly notes from his teacher: "Luke is not getting his work done; he is just not motivated. . . . Luke is restless and inattentive."

Luke also developed behavior problems. After several parent-teacher conferences, he was tested at school, but his IQ was above average. No signs of learning disabilities were found. By spring, Luke was behind in reading, and his teacher recommended that he be retained in second grade. He began second grade again in a large class of twenty-five children. *Surely,* his mother thought, *now he will settle down and enjoy school.* But soon the notes were being sent home again: "Luke is not finishing his seatwork." "Luke can't sit still; he has a hard time staying on a task."

By this time, Luke hated school, and his self-esteem had plummeted. After having him evaluated by a pediatrician and an educational psychologist, his parents were told that he suffered from Attention-Deficit Disorder or ADD.

Like Luke, many children show signs of this "fidgety syndrome." More boys than girls are diagnosed with ADD or ADHD (Attention-Deficit/Hyperactivity Disorder, the term more commonly used now). In 2001, one out of eleven boys, ages three to seventeen, were diagnosed with ADD or ADHD by a doctor or medical professional. Though it's found up to eight times as often in boys as in girls, many girls with ADD without hyperactivity go unnoticed because they're quiet and compliant.

what's the problem?

ADHD is a combination of behaviors that makes it hard for a child to learn in a traditionally organized classroom. Kids with the disorder may interrupt, act up in class, be easily distracted, and go from one uncompleted task to another. They may find it hard to absorb information, and it's more difficult for them to sit still long enough to do everything required by the teacher.

Though the classroom performance of kids with ADHD may be poor, the disorder is not a reflection of low intelligence. These kids have a unique way of processing information and perceiving the world. When their learning needs are met effectively, the sky's the limit on what they can accomplish. Some of the most successful businesspeople have been diagnosed with ADHD.

Despite potential for success, school is a big challenge for these kids. Meg's teachers always described her as "quietly inattentive" and "daydreamy." She was not disruptive in the classroom, but she didn't seem to listen or be "tuned in." Meg missed directions, had trouble getting started, and rarely stuck to a task. Easily distracted, she forgot books or homework assignments, so her schoolwork suffered. On the playground, she had difficulty with team activities. After an exam by her pediatrician and consultation with her teachers and school counselor, she was diagnosed with attention deficit without hyperactivity.

Jake was an overactive child. His mother called him her "little dynamo." From the age of eleven months, he ran around and climbed on everything. In the classroom, he had difficulty sitting still, was distractible, and was always on the go. He seemed to continually drum his fingers or tap his foot. His teacher said he was "driven like a motor." Clumsy, aggressive, and unable to wait his turn, he was left out of the games engaged in by children his age. He was often impulsive and had difficulty organizing his work. When anxious or stressed, Jake became out of control. His problem was attention deficit with hyperactivity.

what are the causes of attention problems?

As with many learning problems, researchers still aren't exactly sure what causes ADD and ADHD. But recent studies point to a strong hereditary and biological component. Kids with these disorders usually have parents or siblings with similar problems. There is also evidence that children who have recurrent middle-ear infections in infancy and as toddlers are much more likely to have auditory processing and attention problems.

Rigid academic demands on elementary school children may also be part of the problem. Doctors report that more children in the first through third grades are being referred for attention problems and hyperactivity as a result of spending a great deal of time at desks doing drills and worksheets and facing rigorous tests, which can create long-term learning problems. "High energy is part of normal childhood. . . . It's perfectly normal for children to be restless, talk a lot or stop paying attention," says learning specialist Priscilla Vail.[1] But if the signs are frequent and are causing problems at school, or if you think there is something wrong, make an appointment with your child's pediatrician.

what ADD is not

Sometimes the label "Attention Deficit" is attached to a child who is overplaced or given work beyond his ability. Children who are developmentally young for their grade level can easily be misdiagnosed by impatient adults. These kids don't need to be on medication; they need time, instruction, patience, and support from teachers and parents. Like the little lion in *Leo the Late Bloomer,* these children will learn, bloom, and shine if their inner time clocks and developmental needs are respected.

There are also other behaviors that look like ADHD. Thyroid disorders can make kids sluggish or hyperactive. Depression or anxiety can make them distractible. Mourning after a major loss such as death or divorce (which can last up to a year) can cause a child to have less concentration, a shortened attention span, and distractibility.

When a child is having attention or other problems in school, parents have to be careful not to attribute everything to neurological problems or disorders, says Dr. David Elkind. He continues,

> The first thing to do is always to look at the child's whole life and what is going on. Is the child totally scheduled and under constant time pressure? Is he having trouble with peers or having trouble with a teacher? Is the family under stress or having problems? Look at all of those things first instead of immediately jumping on a child for being hyperactive and needing medication. I find that too often. When the child is upset or overactive, check out everything else before you consider medication.[2]

It's very important not to self-diagnose or allow a teacher to diagnose but to seek a diagnosis from a physician based on a thorough physical examination, neurodevelopmental assessment, and medical history check. Seek a second opinion if you have any doubt about the diagnosis. Prescriptions made on the basis of a brief interview and exam should be avoided.

"In my experience, a large proportion of children who look like they have 'motivational problems' have undiagnosed special needs," says special needs expert Meredith G. Warshaw.[3] She notes that in addition to ADHD, some of the other hidden disabilities that masquerade as lack of motivation are as follows:

- Auditory processing problems: the ability to process verbal information. Kids suffering from this don't have hearing problems; rather, they have a hard time understanding verbal information, much like trying to learn lessons in a crowded bar with rock music blaring.

- Executive functioning problems: the ability to plan and organize. Children with these problems need explicit instruction in organizational methods and planning their time. It's not a matter of laziness; they're simply late bloomers in this area.

- Dysgraphia: problems with written language. Kids with this disorder have trouble with the mechanics of writing. They may need to start with dictation and then progress to keyboarding. The important thing is not to let the physical limitations get in the way of their expression of ideas.

If you suspect your child's motivational problems are due to one of these or other hidden disabilities, be sure to have him tested to determine exactly what's going on.

how do we help our kids?

"Medication should never be the first alternative," says Norma Sturniolo, M.A., special education coordinator for the schools in Yarmouth, Maine. "Education needs to be the first alternative, followed by modifications in the programs both at school and home to meet the needs of the child. Then if these things are not working, we consider the situation a medical problem."[4]

Although not a cure for all of a child's school problems, in some cases stimulants do seem to improve motor coordination and the ability to focus. "But remember, medication is not a magic pill. It does not make people learn, and it does not make them smarter," says Andy Watry, executive director of the Georgia State Board of Medical Examiners. "All it does technically is to help them in the evaluative thinking process to weed out some of the stray signals so they can focus on a task and not be diverted by every little thing that goes on around them."[5]

Medical literature lists the incidence of ADD as 2 to 3 percent of children. However, 14 percent of today's children are on medication for it, so it seems alarming numbers of children are taking medication for attention disorders when they may not really need it.[6] We need to ask these questions: What can be done to help a child with attention problems without resorting to medication? What can the school do to address the problem? What can parents do at home? Does the problem stem from overplacement, boredom, inappropriate teaching, or an inadequate school environment?

Learn as much as you can about ADHD and other learning

disorders by exploring resources recommended by Children and Adults with Attention-Decifit/Hyperactivity Disorder (CHADD) at www.chadd.org. (There is much misleading information on the Internet, so this is a good place to start for accurate information.)

Homeschooling is an alternative some families are choosing. From early on, Jeremy had problems in school. His teachers described him as disruptive and inattentive. "He doesn't seem to intentionally be out of control; I think it's something chemical," said several of his teachers. After consulting a doctor when Jeremy was in the second grade, his parents put him on medication.

As he grew, the dosage had to be increased and Jeremy began to display severe side effects from the medication—he developed facial tics, suffered from chronic sleeplessness, and acted like a zombie at school. His classroom problems were not abated by the medication. In the third and fourth grades, his teachers said of him, "He disrupts the flow of things" and "He can't keep up." His parents tried placing him in both public and private schools, but the work was overwhelming and he made failing grades in spite of the fact that his achievement test and IQ scores were very high (at the post-high school level in reading and vocabulary).

Social interaction at school was a disaster for Jeremy. He was picked on and ostracized by the other students. His self-esteem plummeted to a low point, and the side effects of the medication made matters even more difficult for him. So when he reached the sixth grade, Jeremy's parents took him off the medication and began homeschooling him. At first his mother worked on filling in the gaps in his knowledge of math, such as how to handle problems in long division, before they could move on to higher math. She integrated literature and history into his schedule. Jeremy was an avid reader and loved science. With the one-to-one instruction provided by his parents, he made progress in all subjects.

Jeremy had the opportunity to develop friendships through youth group activities at church, a homeschool group that met for sports and other events, his local Boy Scout troop, and piano lessons. He also helped with the children his mother cared for in the afternoons when his own learning projects were completed. By age fourteen, Jeremy showed more confidence, enjoyed greater success in his studies, and was more motivated in his schoolwork.

When medication is recommended by your doctor, it needs to be carefully prescribed and regularly monitored at least every six months. The dosage of medication should be the dose that does the job without causing adverse reactions. Therefore, you might see a very large adolescent who only needs a small dosage or a tiny second grader who needs the maximum dose allowable. In addition, modifications such as small group work, individual tutoring, hands-on learning activities at school, and individual and family therapy can work together to benefit the child. Whether or not medication is prescribed, the child with attention problems needs help building his listening skills and attention span and, most of all, boosting his self-worth.

specific ways to help

It's important for us to remember that the child with attention problems does *not* always have difficulty "paying attention." The trouble may be that she's paying *too much* attention to her environment. She lacks the ability to filter out distracting sights, sounds, and even thoughts. She is overwhelmed by the masses of stimuli coming at her, and she lacks the ability to sort out the relevant from the irrelevant. Knowing this, here are a few ways we can help our kids become more successful at filtering out unimportant stimuli and paying attention to the task at hand.

Provide structure at home. Organizing your child's room with his assistance can help bring an inner sense of order and more ability to focus. Use shelves and labels on drawers, a bulletin board with reminders for routines and special activities, and a desk. (Your child may prefer doing homework at the kitchen table near the rest of the family, but beware of the potential for distractions.) He needs a storage box near the door for "school stuff"—his backpack, boots, mittens, and gym clothes. Household routines, boundaries for behavior, consistency, and clear rewards are important. A lack of steady, loving discipline and limit setting in the early years can cause kids to fail to learn self-control, thus aggravating attention problems.

Provide multisensory activities in school and at home. When teachers provide a hands-on task such as building a model after the lesson is presented, it helps the ADHD child concentrate and process the information more effectively. Traditional schools are designed to teach kids who are verbal and auditory learners. Yet kids with attention problems tend to learn in other ways: kinesthetically, musically, tactilely. Talk with your child's teacher about ways your child learns best and how that can be incorporated in the classroom. Work with her to find something your child is good at and make sure she can use that skill in the classroom, such as being responsible for turning on the computers in the morning or drawing a picture of what the class learns each day to be hung on the bulletin board. Be an advocate for your child.

When she's at home, let your active learner make up a cheer for spelling words, bounce a basketball while repeating multiplication tables, or play charades with vocabulary words. Think of ways she can study by seeing, hearing, and doing.

Help her set goals, such as, "After I learn these five states and capitals, I'm going outside to play for a while." For a longer assignment, have the child make a calendar to break the task into steps and place a sticker on each step completed.

Avoid media overload at home. Watching television and playing video games reinforce nonlistening and a short attention span. Instead of media overload, encourage outdoor play (at least an hour a day or more), board games, and puzzles. Playing games will help your child learn to follow directions and sustain attention while trying to reach a concrete goal. Simple games such as Simon Says and I Spy improve listening skills.

Read aloud together. While you read, direct your child's attention to the story line in a high-interest book. Say, for example, "I'm going to read a couple of pages. Something is going to happen to the little girl in the story. I want you to listen for what it is." Then after reading a few pages and hearing his response, ask, "What do you think is going to happen next?"

Prepare your child for what is going to happen and help him develop a sense of sequence and time. Verbal cues such as these help reduce anxiety: "The Smiths are coming for dinner tonight." "You can take a turn with the toy now and your sister can have it this afternoon." "In ten minutes we are leaving for the library." "Soon you can start putting away your Legos."

Keep instructions short and clear. Give them one at a time, gradually increasing the number as the child's attention span grows. Or, if you have several directions for cleaning your child's room, write them on a note.

Build on your child's strengths. Emphasize and reinforce his talents, skills, and positive character traits. Help him become an "expert" at something. What is he good at? What are his special interests? Use the momentum of his enthusiasm to build a string of successes. Find out what he does best and encourage him in it. If your child has an interest in music, get him involved in lessons. Musical activities help children develop timing, memory, and visual and auditory skills—all skills needed by kids with ADHD. Even playing a simple recorder or drumming to music helps a youngster focus his attention and builds mental concentration. Art can also capture his interest and build attention skills.

Most of all, let home be a place where your child knows that in the midst of the challenges of an attention problem, he is unconditionally loved, accepted, and listened to—a place where he can make a mistake and be forgiven. With home and school working together, your child can grow and learn to meet the challenges that lie ahead, take problems in stride, and become productive and happy.

motivation buster #3: single-parent families

I listened as my new neighbor, Carol, poured out her story. After a divorce, she had been left with a demanding job and was trying to get her two boys adjusted in a new school. John, a second grader, was having problems learning to read and was falling behind in class. Aaron, her seventh grader, had tested low in math and language and needed further evaluation. My heart went out to Carol as I recalled my mother, widowed at age thirty-six with six children, and the difficulties she faced that first year as a single parent.

Carol is not alone; the majority of single-parent homes are headed by females. Sometimes kids from such environments have more challenges in school, score lower on achievement tests, and make lower grades than kids from two-parent homes. Most single parents are juggling the demands of a full-time job, household chores, and child care all alone. But they can provide a foundation for achievement in their children's lives.

a background for achievement

Many single parents do a great job of encouraging learning and achievement. For example, Sonia Carson did a marvelous job of motivating her sons. Although she worked three jobs in inner-city Detroit to feed her family, she took them to church weekly, where her son Benjamin caught a vision of becoming a missionary doctor. At school, however, Benjamin was at the bottom of his class and in the lowest reading group. One cause of his problems was poor eyesight. His schoolwork improved once he was fitted with correctly prescribed eyeglasses, but a bigger problem was his lack of motivation. His mother cut her sons' television viewing down to three shows a week. Her boys were required to read two library books a week in addition to completing their homework assignments.

Within eighteen months Benjamin went from last to first place in his class and stayed there throughout high school, receiving a full scholarship to Yale University when he graduated. He went on to graduate from the University of Michigan Medical School and became the chief of pediatric neurosurgery at Johns Hopkins Hospital in Baltimore. He was the first surgeon in medical history to successfully separate head-joined twins. In addition to his career, he takes time to encourage at-risk young people to achieve.

Another great example is Kyle, who derived a lot of confidence from being able to help his mother try new tasks and take initiative. "We've got to change this tire; we'll figure it out together" was his attitude when the tire on their small car went flat. His mother taught him to put oil in the car. He helped her with the household chores, such as keeping his room clean, vacuuming the house, and cleaning out the garage. As a result, he felt he was a worthwhile part of the family and his confidence grew.

He wasn't burdened with too many responsibilities. He had

free time to play soccer and baseball, enjoy friends, and attend church functions. Being a capable kid carried over into his school activities. His teachers reported that he was responsible, mature, and willing to help other students. Though she worked outside the home throughout his childhood, Dixie spent special times with her son and talked to him often.

Single parenting is a tremendous challenge, but let's look at some suggestions single parents have shared that provide a background for learning and success for the single-parent child.

communication

Sometimes opportunities for communication will crop up while you and your child do household chores together—cooking, washing the car, or doing dishes. Dinnertime and bedtime are prime opportunities for sharing. "One of the most helpful times for my family was a one-on-one breakfast hour to keep in touch with where they were and where they wanted to go," says a single mother of three teenagers.

"We tried to have straight communication every morning and evening to avoid surprises," says Allen, a single parent of two girls. "Like a quarterback directing a team, I'd say, 'You're going to be at piano at 3:15, and you'll be at Suzie's. I'll be home at 5:00. Are we all squared away on this?' Then we also gathered at dinner. I don't allow straggling meals where one eats and later another eats in front of the TV. I feel convergence around the table, saying grace, having a sense of order is important."

a network

Providing a support network with a caring neighbor, close family friends and relatives, a grandparent, or a teacher is also helpful. Other adults in the child's life can contribute so much to emotional stability.

"My grandparents provided a very strong, positive relationship. We did things together like fishing, taking long walks, sewing, and reading," says Darien, whose parents were divorced when she was very young. She adds,

> Mother worked full-time while struggling with multiple sclerosis. My mom's cousin spent time with me; she took me shopping, to movies and plays. She taught me about fashion and etiquette. From birth to age seven, I had the same babysitter whose home was out in the country. There I acquired a love for flowers, animals, and the outdoors. Ministers, youth workers, and Young Life leaders also added a lot of stability in crucial times of my life.

Darien, now married and the mother of a son, had an excellent record of achievement in high school and college.

After her husband and daughter died in a car accident, Ellene felt almost overwhelmed with the responsibility of raising her son. She enrolled Jeremy in a Christian school for his seventh-grade year. This was very beneficial, as she explains,

Right away Jeremy began playing on the school's
football team and benefiting from good relationships
with the coaches. He also had a principal and a
whole staff of teachers who cared about him per-
sonally. He gained friends from homes that shared
the same values as ours. There Jeremy has found a
"niche" in this big world where he is accepted and
can excel in positive ways. This is a big encourage-
ment to me.

In addition to his mother, other dads have been good role models for Jeremy and have filled some of his emotional needs. One family friend invited Jeremy to go with him and his son on a National Guard weekend bivouac in the field, a military experience Jeremy will never forget. His soccer coach became a close friend and often invited Jeremy to his home to play computer games with his son and to share their acreage and their love. The family pastor took Jeremy to play golf with him. Times like these have made a tremendous difference in Jeremy's life.

getting help

Sometimes a single parent needs extra help, as Gail, a secretary and single parent, can attest to:

After my husband left, Jennifer, eight years old,
seemed so helpful with the three-year-old. I was

having a difficult time, feeling sorry for myself, depressed, trying to get our life together. After two months of school, the teacher called me and told me that Jennifer was a very angry girl. She took her anger out on everyone and everything at school. The teacher felt she needed help and recommended the school counselor. What I learned is that we forget sometimes that our children suffer through losses just like we do, and because they want to protect their moms, they try to be big and not show they're hurting too. I found we need to be aware of our children's emotions and what they go through.

Parents shouldn't be shy about getting the necessary support they may need from a pastor, a counselor, their family, or their friends. As the child is helped with her emotions, she can be free to concentrate on her studies at school.

getting involved

"That first fall the girls and I were alone together, it hit me that we had a homework problem," says Allen. He continues,

Neither daughter wanted to study. One was totally disorganized, losing papers and waiting until the night before a big project was due to announce it.

We talked about what a good assignment notebook looks like, and I had the girls keep it up daily and plan ahead on projects. I put some of my evening meetings aside to spend more time with the girls. Their spelling was very weak, so I'd ask early in the week, "What are your spelling words? Let's put them on the refrigerator and go over them." By being involved with their studies, we saw grades come way up for the term.

Children thrive on order and structure. Allen shared how important it was in his case to reestablish a family routine and have a regular schedule for eating, sleeping, playing, and studying. They found that setting some time aside to just have fun together —taking a trip to the zoo or going on a picnic in the park—is important, even with all the responsibilities.

Getting involved with your kids' teachers can help tremendously as well. Even when you can't get to your kids' school frequently, written communication with the teacher can develop rapport without taking you away from your job. As a former teacher, I can tell you that the effect of a positive note from a parent can be amazing. I rarely received notes from parents, and when I did, they were usually to point out a problem. If you take the time to write a positive note of appreciation, your child's teacher will remember it and may be more aware of your child and your willingness to be cooperative with the teacher's efforts. These days, most teachers check their e-mail frequently, even every day. Why not make it a point to e-mail your children's teachers once every couple of weeks with a positive comment or a question?

after-school matters

All parents are aware of the need for younger children to be supervised after school. But we usually breathe a sigh of relief when kids reach junior high, and we feel less pressure to supervise them at all times. Unfortunately, studies and anecdotal evidence over the last few years have taught us that kids actually need adults present all the way through high school, and this can be particularly difficult for single parents. You might consider looking into a high-quality after-school program at a neighbor's house or at your child's school, YMCA, or local church where recreation, a snack, and homework help are available. Or, you could hire a college student or retired teacher to provide some inexpensive after-school homework help and company.

Also, remember that kids love it when you take an active role in their activities, especially in junior and senior high school. Try to attend their sporting events, recitals, debates, and drama events when you can. Kids may never admit they want you there—but when the big day comes, they always look for you!

With these ingredients, single-parent children can do far more than just survive their school years. They can *achieve* and grow in skills and confidence to tackle all the challenges that lie ahead.

motivation buster #4: burnout

Jason's second-grade teacher handed him his spelling test with the grade D written across the top in red ink. "Don't you think you can do better than this, Jason?" his teacher asked as she posted the scores on the bulletin board.

Jason slumped down into his chair and lowered his head. The bell rang, and the other children ran out to recess, chattering and pushing. Jason chewed his bottom lip as he crumpled up his test paper and stuck it in his notebook.

When Jason got home that afternoon, his mother met him at the door. "Hi, Jason! How did you do on your spelling test today?"

"I don't know," answered Jason, his blue eyes avoiding her gaze. He unloaded his books and headed for the refrigerator.

His mother sifted through the papers jammed into his notebook until she came to the spelling test. "A D! Jason, this is terrible. How could you make a D?" She frowned, smoothing the wrinkles out of his paper. "*School?* You mean you couldn't even spell *school?*"

"I hate school anyway," Jason mumbled between bites of an apple as he quickly made his way out the patio door. "I'm going to ride bikes with Brian."

"Oh no, you're not. You've got only thirty minutes to do your math homework before I take you to karate. And tonight's the

Scout banquet, and then Dad's going to help you with your social studies project."

Jason stamped away to his room and slammed the door. Throughout the coming weeks, his grades dropped to Fs, and his reading skills were reported to be below grade level. Being grounded from PlayStation, TV, and his bike didn't help. Recurrent nightmares disturbed his sleep, and he woke up tired every morning. Frustrated with his failure, his parents sought help in teacher conferences and from an outside reading specialist. Gradually they began to unravel his problem.

Jason had begun preschool and kindergarten as a happy, intelligent child. His preschool and kindergarten teachers emphasized formal instruction in reading and arithmetic, and his parents were confident that this early foundation would give Jason a head start in school. Both of them were high-achieving professionals who were anxious to give their son the best possible educational beginning. They were eager for him to succeed in school, piano and karate lessons, soccer, basketball, and Little League baseball.

But at eight years of age, he was exhausted from lessons and activities every day after school. Jason was a sad-looking, stressed child who had very little motivation for learning. He had trouble keeping up with his papers and books and was failing in his schoolwork.

Jason was the victim of a competitive, overly academic school system, which placed lots of emphasis on worksheets and tests and not enough on hands-on activities and concrete learning. He was pressured at home by conscientious parents who wanted him to do well in everything. He was stressed by a lack of free time to play, explore his own interests, and develop friendships. So at the early age of eight, Jason was, in fact, burned out.

Here is some advice his parents followed to relieve his pressure:

- Emphasize what is being learned both in and out of the classroom rather than test scores and report card grades. (We covered this in depth in chapter 5.) Jason's parents stopped showing disapproval for a low grade; instead, they asked, "Are you having any problems? How can we help?"

- Help him organize his studies and materials. Jason's parents helped color code a folder for each subject and made a calendar with his homework assignments to display prominently in his room. This helped build in Jason a sense of personal responsibility. And being organized, he had more energy and motivation to put into schoolwork.

- Deal with overscheduling. His parents decided to give Jason the choice of pursuing one favorite activity (he chose soccer) and dropping the others so he could have some unstructured time to play in the neighborhood, ride his bicycle, or have a friend over after school. His dad set aside time on Saturdays to go with Jason to the park, kick the soccer ball around, and just talk. When he wasn't running from activity to activity, he had time to help with some chores, walk the dog, and take out the trash. A retired teacher who lived down the street met with Jason weekly to build his basic skills through a variety of interesting, creative activities.

These small changes made a big difference. Jason's schoolwork gradually improved, and by Christmas of the following year he was reading on grade level. By the fourth grade, he was a solid B student, slept better, and was happier at school, at home, and with his friends. And he thoroughly enjoyed soccer.

what causes burnout?

Although burnout can take place at any age, it is occurring more frequently in younger children. One of the major causes of premature burnout is placing children in pressured academic situations, often as early as age four through six, with hours devoted to desk time, worksheets, and tests. Tufts University psychologist Dr. David Elkind warns against rigid preschool and early elementary programs that emphasize rote learning, ignore young children's developmental needs, and put them at risk due to stress and learning problems.[1]

My daughter-in-law Tiffany wisely decided not to schedule her daughter Caitlin for any extracurricular activities for the first half of kindergarten. This gave Caitlin a chance to adjust and have playtime and lots of playdates with friends. She had a good transition and wasn't overwhelmed by the increased demands of kindergarten. When the second half of the school year began, she went back to dance classes after school and enjoyed them with renewed enthusiasm.

Another cause for burnout is overscheduling kids. Many children are involved in some type of planned after-school activity every day of the week. Their schedules are crammed with tennis and dance lessons, competitive sports, and other responsibilities in addition to homework. Structure, rather than spontaneity, marks the lives of many children today. Some structure is helpful, and the activities themselves may be valuable. But overstructuring kids' lives to the point that they don't have time to relax, read for leisure, daydream, or play leads to burnout.

Some kids seem to be able to handle a hectic schedule, while others are stressed by it. To evaluate how your child handles things, you might ask these questions:

- Does your child seem to thrive on structured activities?

- Is she eager for scheduled lessons?

- Can she handle this extra involvement along with her regular homework and family responsibilities without feeling pressured, losing sleep, or becoming cranky and irritable?

Also, we can consider whether the activity is being chosen for the sake of the child or simply to fulfill our own aspirations. If I always wanted to tap dance and play musical instruments but couldn't, I'd better not force that dream on my children. It's one thing to introduce them to opportunities to learn and quite another to make those activities compulsory.[2] If you suspect your child may be overscheduled, I highly recommend you read the book *The Over-Scheduled Child: Avoiding the Hyper-Parenting Trap* by Alvin Rosenfeld, M.D., and Nicole Wise.

What can we do to avoid the overscheduling that leads to burnout?

- *Relax the schedule.* We need to give children of all ages opportunities for unstructured play, reflection, and rest. The key is to balance planned after-school activities with unstructured time. All young people need at least an hour a day of free time and outdoor play. What if they get bored? Boredom isn't the worst thing in the world, and it might lead to climbing or swinging in the backyard, engaging in creative daydreaming, drawing, or even discovering their own interests!

- *Slow down and take time.* Sometimes there are too many things going on in a child's life. We're all so busy. Taking time to just listen to your child's fears or dreams can reduce stress and avoid burnout.

- *Be aware of the signs of stress and burnout in kids.* These signs can be sudden changes in attitude or behavior (your happy kid has become hostile, your cooperative son has become uncooperative), declining grades, difficulty concentrating, sleeping problems, a lack of desire to go to school, depression, anxiety, or physical complaints, such as headaches, stomachaches, excess fatigue, or loss of appetite. One of these signs might not be cause for alarm, but a cluster of signs would suggest that your child may be overly pressured by the demands placed on her at school and home.

Michael, a first grader I know, was bright and talented and always tried hard to do his best. He was involved in intensive gymnastics practice three days a week for two and a half hours each day (in addition to church, school, and Scouts), and most of his Saturdays were spent in five or six hours of competition. He had little free time. His teacher told Michael's parents of her concerns about his classroom behavior. He was always worried about his work. He feared making a mistake. He was fretful that something terrible would happen if an assignment was not done at the exact time required. His parents realized that part of Michael's problem was the constant pressure to perform and the overstructured life he was leading.

"It's easy to get caught up in the competition," Michael's mom explained. "You can't sit out a year or everyone will pass you by. The whole program is oriented to produce superstars and winners." It was a difficult decision, but after talking with him, Michael's parents decided to take him out of competitive gymnastics at the end of the school year. He still worked out for fun at the YMCA and with friends and took a summer gymnastics workshop. He started participating in a mime group, which made use of his physical and coordination talents. He was less worried and stressed, although he still worked hard and enjoyed his activities.

As we choose activities and provide resources that meet our children's needs in their early years and find a good balance between structured and unstructured time, we can help them avoid the pitfalls of burnout and stay motivated for the adventures of learning and life.

motivation and success

One day recently I was talking with D. L. Gheen, pediatrician and specialist in learning and behavior problems, about how the secret to motivation is success.

Over the years, many parents have asked him, "How do I motivate my kids?" He responds by asking them whether their kids are having very many successes—in school, in sports, or even in keeping their room clean. Often the parents have a hard time identifying areas in which their kids are achieving.

We both agreed that it's not very motivating to go out and fail every day. Neither is it motivating to have parents, teachers, and other adults who do everything for a child and don't require much effort or responsibility from him. Kids need to experience some small triumphs regularly—and have these little victories recognized—to stay motivated for school, sports, and family obligations. They need these accomplishments to be *theirs alone*—something they've achieved all by themselves. A taste of success leads to a desire for more success, which is a very powerful motivator in school and in life.

Hopefully, that's the message you've taken from this book. I've tried to convey a multitude of ways to help your children experience those positive, competent feelings that spur them on. Growing up is hard work. The number of things a child must achieve, master, and remember in his first eighteen years is staggering. If he doesn't get an ongoing sense of his own accomplishment and a belief that he actually *can do it,* it's so easy to just give up trying. By helping your child experience some degree of success in the different things he tries, you're giving him the best possible chance of being a motivated kid. Success leads to motivation, and motivation leads to more success. This builds momentum, and as I discussed in the first chapter, developing momentum is crucial to a motivated kid.

As a parent, you're the person in the best position to kindle your child's motivation. I hope some of the suggestions in this book are helpful to you, inspiring you to ignite the fire of motivation in your children and create in them a love of learning and the positive, "can-do" attitude they'll need to achieve in the classroom and in the world in which they live.

notes

chapter one — what is motivation?

1. Nancy Paulu, "Motivation—Helping Your Child Through Early Adolescence," U.S. Department of Education, http://www.ed.gov/parents/academic/help/adolescence/partx4.html (accessed February 24, 2004).

chapter two — the first building block: relationship

1. Dr. Arthur M. Bodin (past president, Division of Family Psychology of the American Psychological Association, a senior research fellow at the Mental Research Institute), in an interview with the author, 1989.
2. Eve Bither (Commissioner of Education for the state of Maine), in an interview with the author.
3. Edith Schaeffer, in an interview with the author.
4. Dr. Yamamoto (professor, University of Colorado), in an interview with the author.
5. Dorothy Corkille Briggs, *Your Child's Self-Esteem: Step-by-Step Guidelines for Raising Responsible, Productive, Happy Children* (New York: Doubleday, 1975), p. 273.

chapter three — the second building block: a good example

1. Dr. Arthur M. Bodin, in an interview with the author.
2. Jim Trelease, *The Read-Aloud Handbook* (New York: Penguin Books, 2000).
3. Jennifer Jacobson, in an interview with the author, March 1989.

4. Frank Smith, *Essays into Literacy: Selected Papers and Some Afterthoughts* (Portsmouth: Heinemann Educations Books, 1983), p. 100.

chapter four — the third building block: expectations

1. Vonnette Bright, "Women Today" radio program, Campus Crusade for Christ Ministry, July 1997.
2. Dr. Carol Kelly, in an interview with the author.
3. David Lowenstein, Ph.D., "Motivation and Your Child," *Mom & Dad's Manual,* http://www.clubtheo.com/momdad/html/dlmotivation.html (accessed February 25, 2004).
4. Norman Vincent Peale, "The Stupendous Power of Hope," *Plus: The Magazine of Positive Thinking,* May 1995, pp. 19-20.
5. Dr. H. William Mitchell, *Homemade* 22, no. 11 (Nov. 1988), published by Family Concern.
6. John Drescher, *Seven Things Children Need* (Scottdale, Pa.: Herald Press, 1976), p. 59.
7. Nancy Paulu, "Motivation—Helping Your Child Through Early Adolescence," U.S. Department of Education, http://www.ed.gov/parents/academic/help/adolescence/partx4.html (accessed February 24, 2004).
8. Dorothy Corkille Briggs, *Your Child's Self-Esteem: Step-by-Step Guidelines for Raising Responsible, Productive, Happy Children* (New York: Doubleday, 1975), p. 272.

chapter five — the fourth building block: a healthy perspective

1. Sam Goldstein, "Paying Attention to the Inflation of Worry," http://www.samgoldstein.com/template.php?page=postings&type=articles&id=50 (accessed February 25, 2004).
2. Thomas Schultz Publications, *Parents and Teenagers Newsletter* 1, no. 1 (1989): 1.
3. Dr. Arthur M. Bodin, in an interview with the author.
4. "Kids Admit Cheating, Drinking, and Lying," *Arizona Daily Star,* October 16, 2000, www.azstarnet.com.

5. Interview with high school principal, 1988. Interview conducted in confidentiality; name withheld by mutual agreement.
6. Interview with middle school teacher, 1988. Interview conducted in confidentiality; name withheld by mutual agreement.
7. "Cheating," The Nemours Foundation, http://www.kidshealth.org/kid/feeling/school/cheating.html (accessed January 13, 2004).
8. Bodin, interview.
9. Bodin, interview.
10. Dr. David Elkind, in an interview with the author.
11. Edith Schaeffer, in an interview with the author.

chapter six — motivation booster #1: patience

1. Dr. Louise Bates Ames, *Don't Push Your Preschooler* (New York: Harper & Row, 1980), p. 203.
2. See *Touchpoints: Your Child's Emotional and Behavioral Development* by Dr. T. Berry Brazelton (Perseus Publishing, 1992) or *Your Two-Year-Old, Your Three-Year-Old* series by Dr. Louise Bates Ames.
3. Ames, p. 201.
4. Ames, p. 8.
5. Vicky Mlyniec, "Reading, Writing, and Relaxation: How Slowing Down Speeds Learning," *Family Circle,* September 2, 2003, p. 78.
6. Rudolf Flesch, ed., *The Book of Unusual Quotations* (New York: Harper & Row, 1957), p. 204.
7. Robert Kraus, *Leo the Late Bloomer* (New York: Windmill Books, 1971).

chapter seven — motivation booster #2: storytelling

1. U.S. Department of Education, *What Works: Research About Teaching and Learning* (Washington, D.C.: Government Printing Office, 1987), p. 25.
2. Vance Packard, *A Nation of Strangers* (New York: David McKay, Inc., 1972).
3. Adapted version by Barbara McBride-Smith, Stillwater, Oklahoma. Used with permission.

4. My thanks to Oklahoma teacher and storyteller Vivian Nida for these questions.
5. These questions were adapted from William Zimmerman, *Instant Oral Biographies* (New York: Guarionex Press, Ltd., 1982).

chapter eight — motivation booster #3: developing curiosity

1. Dr. David Elkind, in an interview with the author.
2. Dr. Jane Healy (educational psychologist and author of *Your Child's Growing Mind*) and Dr. Stanley Greenspan (author of *The Growth of the Mind*), in a discussion with the author.
3. Dr. Stanley Greenspan, in an interview with the author.
4. Namsoo Shin and Steven McGee, "Identifying Questions to Investigate: A Research Question Should Pique Students' Curiosity," www.cotf.edu/vdc/entries/motivation.html (accessed January 2004).
5. Dorothy Corkille Briggs, *Your Child's Self-Esteem: Step-by-Step Guidelines for Raising Responsible, Productive, Happy Children* (New York: Doubleday, 1975), pp. 264-265.
6. Greenspan, interview.

chapter nine — motivation booster #4: learning about the world

1. Kelly Hagan (college student), in an interview with the author, 1989.
2. Some of these suggestions are adapted from "Host Family Ministry," National Student Ministries, 127 Ninth Avenue North, Nashville, TN 37234.

chapter ten — motivation booster #5: the attitudes of responsibility and optimism

1. Bonnie Runyan McCullough and Susan Walker Monson, *401 Ways to Get Your Kids to Work at Home* (New York: St. Martin's Press, 1981), p. vii.

2. Dr. Martin E. P. Seligman's book *The Optimistic Child: A Proven Program to Safeguard Children Against Depression and Build Lifelong Resilience* (Perennial, 1996) is a good guide for parents facing negativity and pessimism. Some of the concepts in this chapter are adapted from a live presentation by Dr. Seligman on the need to teach children optimism.
3. Tom Carpenter, "Three Secret Motivational Methods of Thomas Edison," *SYSEDCO*, http://www.sysedco.com/library/articles/ThreeSecretMotivationalMethodsofThomasEdison.asp (accessed February 26, 2004).
4. Mark Water, comp., *The New Encyclopedia of Christian Quotations* (Grand Rapids, Mich.: Baker, 2000), p. 980.

chapter eleven — motivation buster #1: perfectionism

1. Miriam Adderholdt-Elliott, "What's Bad About Being Good?" *The Education Digest*, November 1988, p. 27.
2. John Stossel, "Relentless Pursuits: Pushing for Perfection Can Cause Real Problems for Kids," http://abcnews.go.com/sections/2020/DailyNews/stossel_familyfix_020920.html (accessed January 13, 2004).
3. Dr. Carol Kelly, in an interview with the author.
4. Dr. Carol Kelly, in an interview with the author.
5. Stossel, "Relentless Pursuits."

chapter twelve — motivation buster #2: attention problems

1. Priscilla Vail, "What's Wrong with My Child?" *Ladies Home Journal*, April 1992, pp. 98-100.
2. Dr. David Elkind, in an interview with the author.
3. Meredith G. Warshaw, M.S.S., M.A., "Uniquely Gifted: Motivation Problem or Hidden Disability?" http://uniquelygifted.org/motivation.htm (accessed February 24, 2004).
4. Norma Sturniolo, M.A., in an interview with the author.
5. Andy Watry, in an interview with the author.
6. Dr. D. L. Gheen (pediatrician and ADD specialist in Edmond, Oklahoma), in an interview with the author.

chapter fourteen — motivation buster #4: burnout

1. Dr. David Elkind, in an interview with the author.
2. Dr. Arthur M. Bodin, in an interview with the author.

about the author

Cheri Fuller is an award-winning author, speaker, and mother of three grown children. Her thirty published books include *School Starts at Home; Talkers, Watchers, and Doers; Opening Your Child's Nine Learning Windows; How to Grow a Young Music Lover; Extraordinary Kids* (coauthored with Louise Tucker Jones); and *The Mom You're Meant to Be*. She speaks to parents, teachers, and mothers' and women's groups both in the U.S. and internationally and has appeared on national radio and TV programs. Hundreds of Cheri's articles have appeared in *Family Circle, ParentLife, Guideposts, Focus on the Family, Living with Teenagers, CHILD*, and many other magazines. She has worked with children for over thirty years and lives with her husband in Oklahoma.

For information on her speaking and other resources, visit her website at www.cherifuller.com.

Other books in the SCHOOL SAVVY KIDS series by Cheri Fuller.

Talkers, Watchers, and Doers

Create a tailor-made learning environment for each of your children, equipping them with specialized study skills to match their unique personalities.
1-57683-599-5

School Starts at Home

Discover how you can foster a stimulating, creative environment for your children by modeling a love of learning at home.
1-57683-600-2

To get your copies, visit your local bookstore.

LC 3/10
TC 3
TRO 6/11 -5x